Theory and Improvisation for the Modern Mandolinist

Volume 1

Building a Foundation

by Tommy Norris

Online Audio www.melbay.com/30617MEB

WWW.MELBAY.COM

Table of Contents

Introduction

Hello and welcome to the world of mandolin improvisation! This two-part series will help improve your improvisation and writing, as well as increase your overall familiarity with the instrument itself.

This first book, *Building a Foundation*, will give you the basic skills needed to improvise over chord progressions found in all styles of music. As long as you can play notes and simple chords, you can use this book! It starts with the most basic concepts of theory and improvisation, and slowly adds to these a little at a time. Each chapter presents scales in three different ways: standard notation, tablature, and fretboard charts. At the end of every chapter there are sample solos and progressions for practice. This book includes access to online audio containing recordings of each of these progressions, as well as other progressions in the appendix. Practice playing along with these recordings after each chapter.

Tablature

Below are two measures of standard notation and tab in one stave system. The numbers on the bottom are tab, and correspond exactly to the music written above. The lines of the tab represent the different strings of the mandolin; with the bottom line being **G**, followed by **D**, **A**, and the top line, **E**. The numbers tell you what fret to place your finger on, with 0 representing the open string.

Fingerings: Unless otherwise noted, for open position use your index finger for the 1st and 2nd frets, middle finger for the 3rd and 4th frets, ring finger for the 5th and 6th frets, and pinky for the 7th and 8th frets. Alternate fingerings will be marked in parenthesis above the tab with numbers corresponding to which fingers to use (Index =1 , Middle =2, Ring =3, Pinky =4).

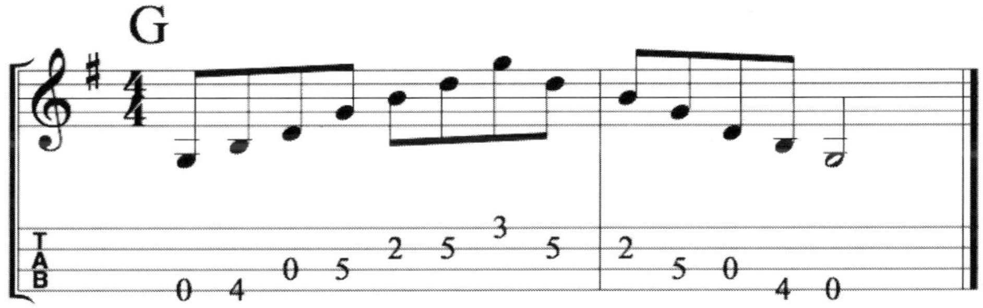

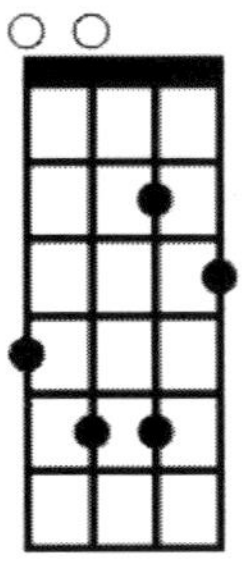

Fretboard Charts

Fretboard charts show the mandolin fretboard as you would see it if you held the mandolin in front of you and looked straight at it. The charts will help you visualize the different arpeggios and scales. The vertical lines represent the strings (left to right: G, D, A, E) and the horizontal lines are frets. The dots show you where to place your fingers, with the white circles representing the open strings that you play. The charts in this book are for scales, so you play each note separately starting with the lowest sounding note. (In this case open G). This chart represents the same scale as the tab above.

Basic Chord Theory

When playing a solo, you will most likely be playing over a chord or chord progression. Understanding how these chords and progressions work is an invaluable tool when creating melodies and improvising solos.

Chords are built from major scales, which are the notes of a musical key played in sequence. For example, in the key of G major, if you start with the note G and play the rest of the notes in the key, you have the G major scale. After all the notes in the key are played, they repeat again starting on G an octave* higher.

G Major Scale

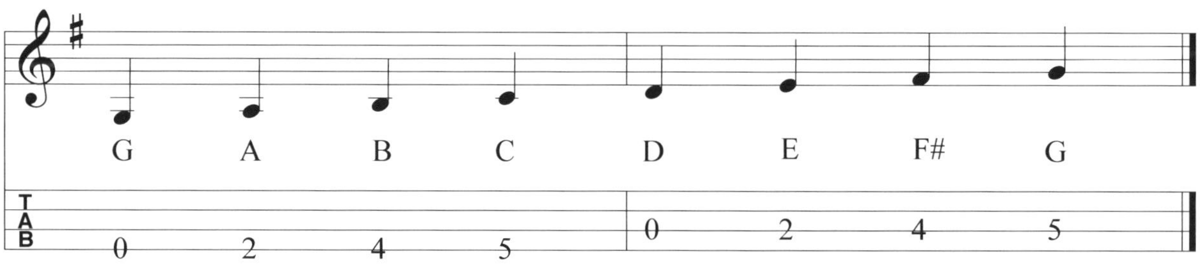

Triads

A chord consists of three or more notes played simultaneously. When a chord has only three notes, it is known as a **triad**. The three notes are called the 1st, the 3rd, and the 5th, named for the position they occupy in the major scale.

In the key of G major, you'll encounter the following triads made up of notes from the G major scale:

Triads in the Key of G:

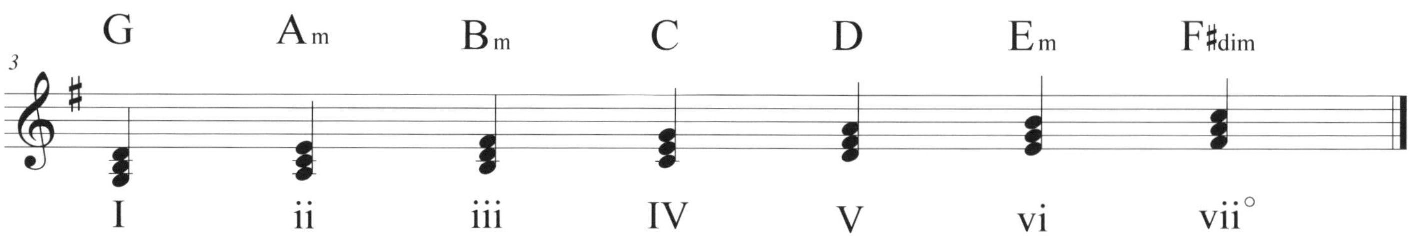

* The same note repeated in a higher or lower register.

Basic Chord Theory Continued

Notice that each chord has a Roman numeral under it. These numbers are used to represent the chord's function in the key.

Most progressions start on the **I** chord, then play any of the other chords, and end on the **I** chord, most likely preceded by a **V** chord.

One thing to remember is that while different keys have different chords, they also share some of the same chords. For example: In the key of G there is a D chord which is the **V**. In the key of A, there is also a D chord but it is the **IV** chord.

These Roman numerals are also useful for writing out chord progressions without specifying a key. You could easily play the progression in any key. For example, here is a common chord progression:

I - IV - V - I

In the key of G, the **I** chord would be a G, the **IV** chord a C, and the **V** chord a D.

In the key of D, the **I** chord would be a D, the **IV** chord a G, and the **V** chord an A.

Lowercase numerals denote minor chords. For example, The **ii** chord in the key of G would be A minor. The lowercase numeral **vii°** hypertext **°** indicates a diminished triad.

Chords can also be altered from their natural tonality in a key, for example, making the **IV** chord in the key of G (C Major) a **iv** chord (C Minor).

When improvising or jamming, you are expected to have memorized the chords in each key. Use the appendix section at the end of this book to help you learn the different keys.

Enharmonics

Notes with **accidentals** (sharps and flats) each have what is called an **enharmonic counterpart.** These are the same notes, just written differently- depending on the key. For example, the notes **B♭** and **A♯** are the same note. The note **B♭** is in the key of **F**, which is a flat-bearing key and **A♯** is found in the key of **B,** a sharp-bearing key. It is important to keep shared enharmonic tones in mind when you are learning different keys. Below are all the notes with accidentals written out with their enharmonic counterparts:

C | C♯/D♭ | D | D♯/E♭ | E | F | F♯/G♭ | G | G♯/A♭ | A | A♯/B♭ | B

1. Major Triads and Chord Tones

A great way to begin learning how to improvise is by playing **chord triads**. When you have these notes under your fingers, you have a good homebase to come back to if you get lost at any point.

The idea here is to understand what the member chord tones are for each of the different triads. No matter what song you play, if you know the triad chord tones for the current chord being played, you can play those notes and they will <u>always</u> work!

Here are the major triad chord arpeggios for G, C and D. Practice these repeatedly until you are comfortable enough to play the notes in any order. The goal is to be able to look at your fretboard, and visualize where the notes are before you even play them.

The following diagrams start on the lowest note of the chord that can be played on the mandolin, which is not always the **root** of the chord, i.e., G in the G chord, C in the C chord, etc. The roots themselves are marked with an R in each stave system.

G

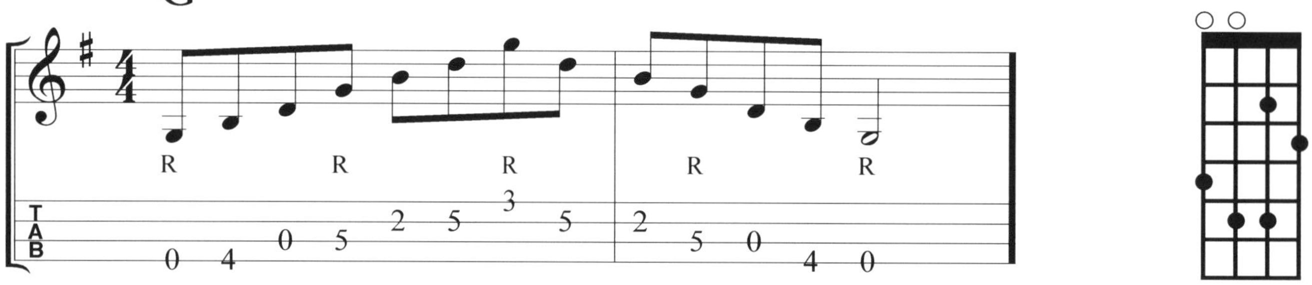

C

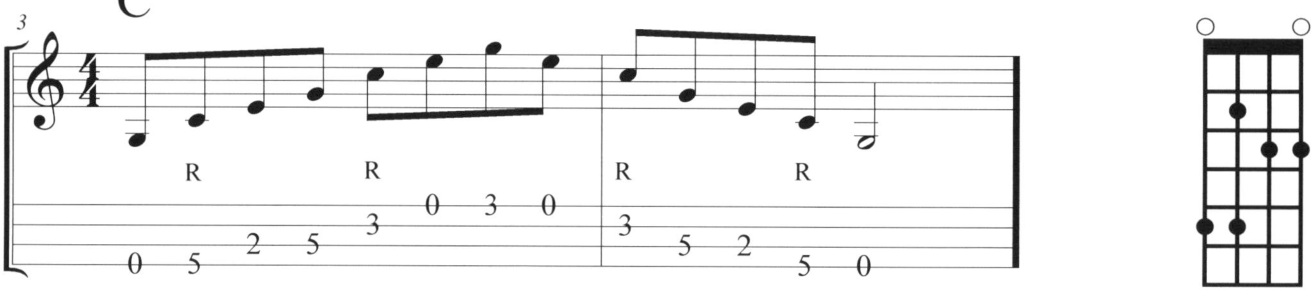

D

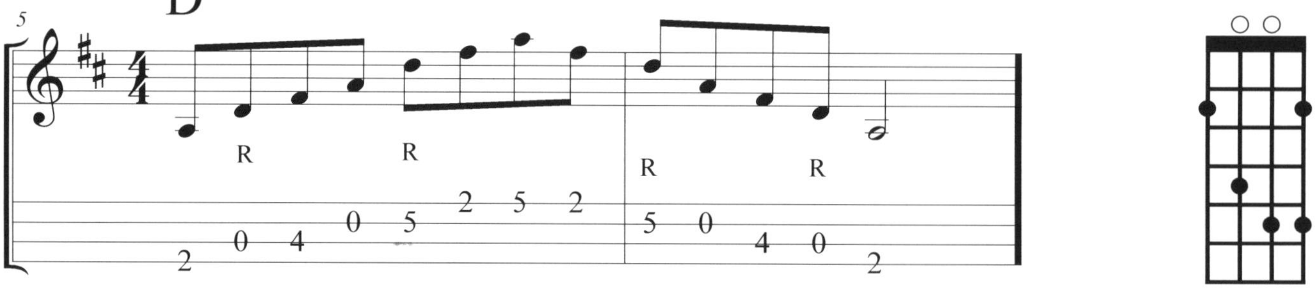

Major Triad Practice Progression

Below is a simple chord progression using the triads we learned on the last page, as well as a short sample solo over these chords using only chord tones. Soloing with just chord tones might not sound the greatest, but for now, you are practicing the ability to easily find these basic tones when we add more notes later.

Learn the solo below, and then practice writing your own solos using only chord tones. Remember to change the chord tones you play depending on what chord is sounding!

When you are comfortable enough, try playing along with the backing track (or another player!) and improvising your own solo.

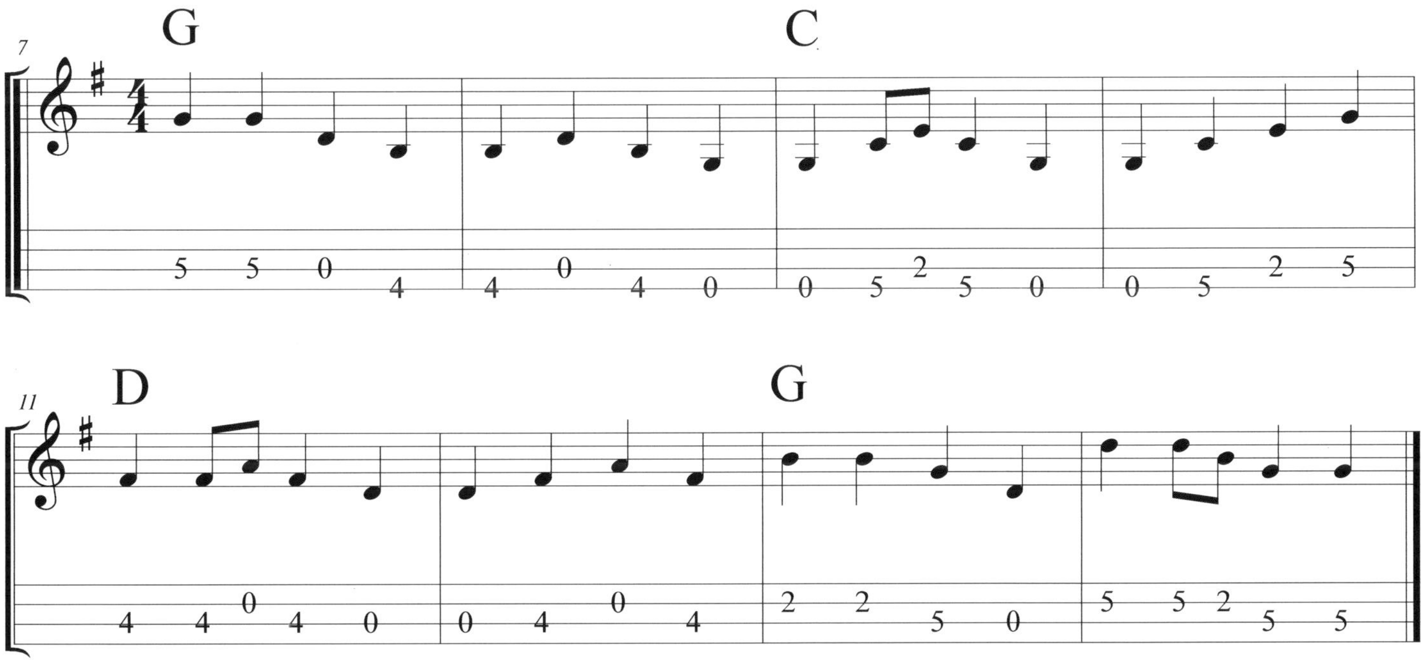

Solo Tip: Common Tones

When learning these triads, you might have noticed that a few of the same notes occur in more than one chord. It is good to be aware of these, so when you get to faster chord progressions, you can play one note over multiple chords if needed. This technique is used in the "Practice Progression" above from the end of the 2nd measure into the 3rd measure. The common tone between the G and the C chord is "G".

2. Pentatonic Scales

Now that we've learned major triads and how to use them in improvisation, let's add a couple of notes to each of the arpeggios and turn them into "Pentatonic" (five-note) scales.

Pentatonic scales are used in all kinds of folk and popular music around the world. Learn the scales from the figures below and remember to try to visualize where the scale notes are on the fretboard. Just like the triads from last chapter, these scales are meant to be played only over the chord they represent. For example: Play the G pentatonic scale over G chords, C pentatonic over C chords, etc.

Keep in mind the original triad chord tones as you learn these pentatonic scales. The goal is to think about the pentatonic scales as chord triads with a couple of added notes.

G

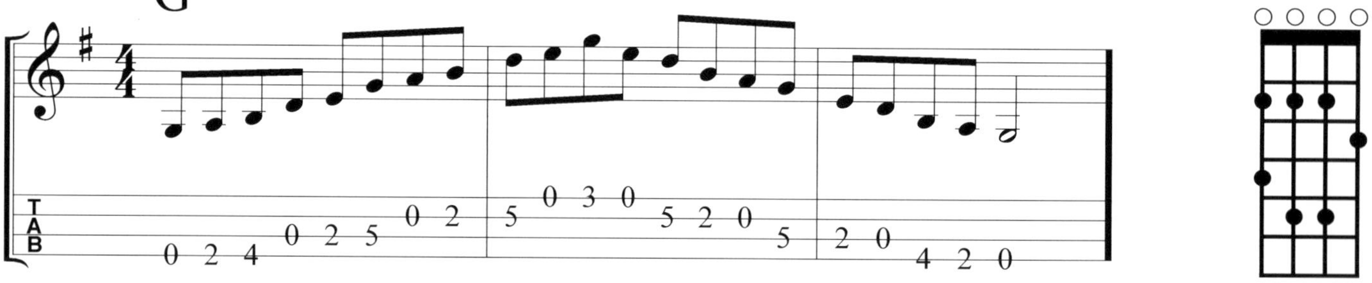

C

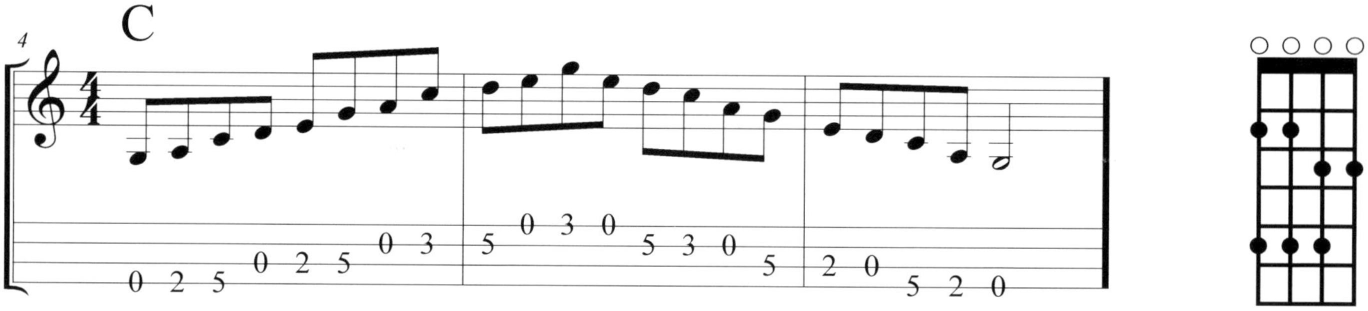

D

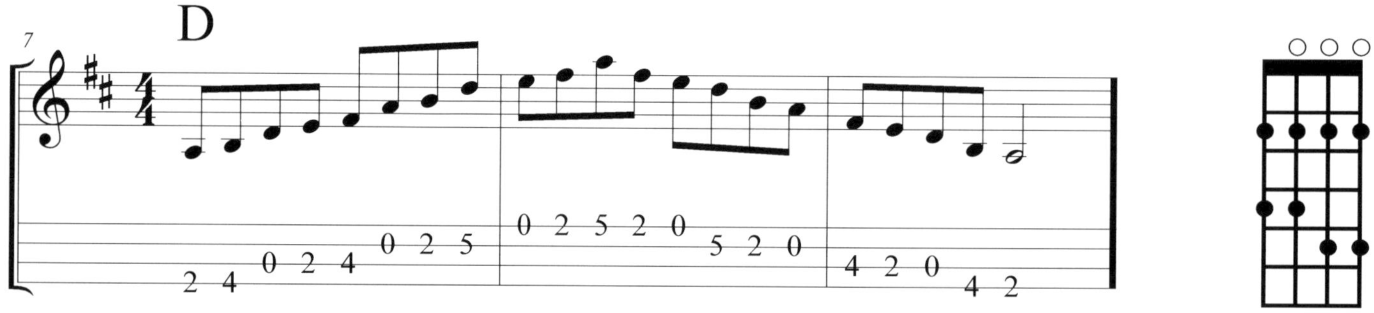

Pentatonic Song Example: "Angeline the Baker"

Below is the first section from the popular fiddle tune "Angeline the Baker".

This song uses only pentatonic scale notes for the melody.

Learn the melody below and then try to write your own solo using just pentatonic scales.

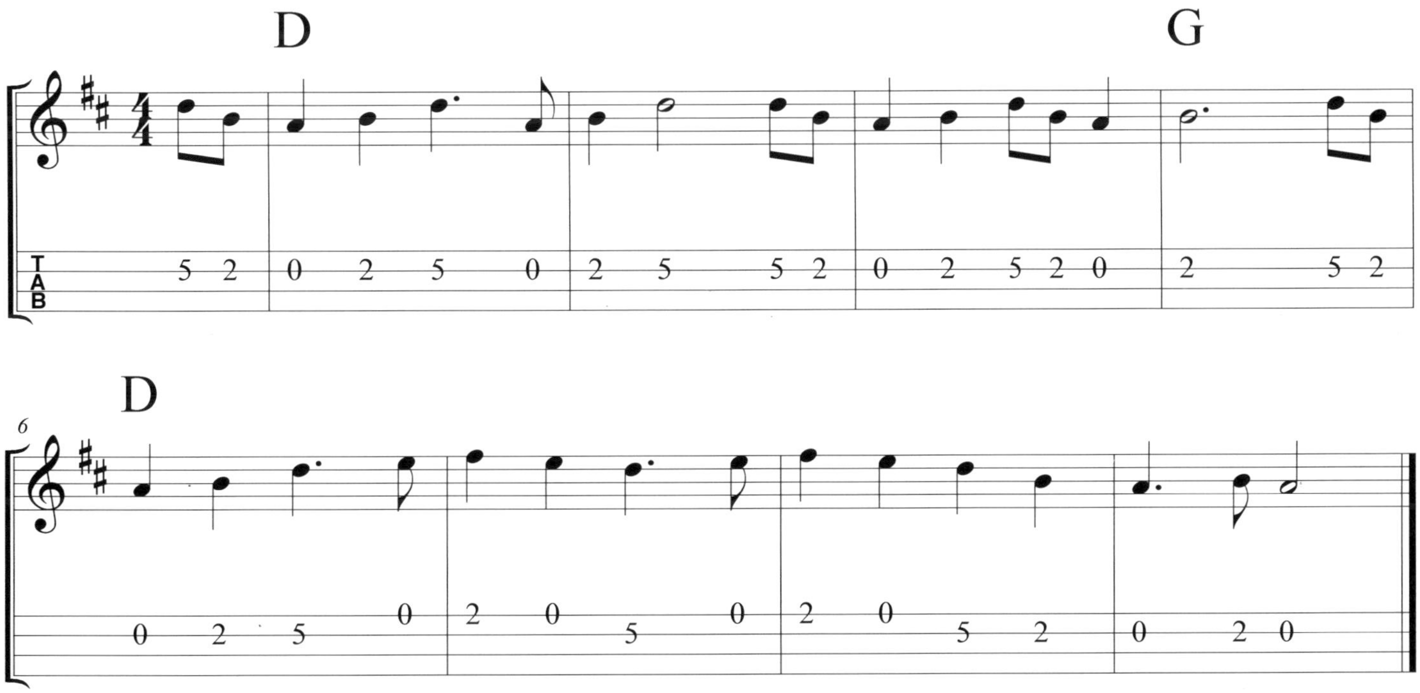

Solo Tip: Pentatonic Common Tones

Just like triads, pentatonic scales have notes shared between them. The two different notes played over the G chord (in measure 4) fit both the D and G pentatonic scales. It is a good idea to familiarize yourself with these and other common tones so switching between scales will become easier.

Pentatonic Practice Progression

Here is the same practice progression used in the last chapter with a sample solo using pentatonic scales.

As in the previous chapter, learn the solo written below and then practice writing and improvising your own solo.

Solo Tip: Focusing on Chord Tones

Notice that the solo written above uses pentatonic scales, but still focuses on landing on triad chord tones.

Every longer note in the solo is a chord tone. The other two pentatonic scale notes are used as **passing tones** leading up or down to a chord tone. This is great rule of thumb to keep in mind when writing and improvising solos.

No matter how complex your solo gets, always try to land on the basic chord tones.

3. Basic Minor Chords

Up to this point we have only focused on major chords, so let's look at a couple of minor chords. Minor triads are different from major triads in that they have a lowered 3rd (♭3). They are denoted with a lowercase **m** next to the chord name.

Em and Am chords are often used in the keys of C and G, and are great chords to learn to compliment the G, C and D chords we learned earlier.

Here are the triads for Em and Am. Learn these minor triads the same way you learned the major triads, and look for common notes between them.

Em

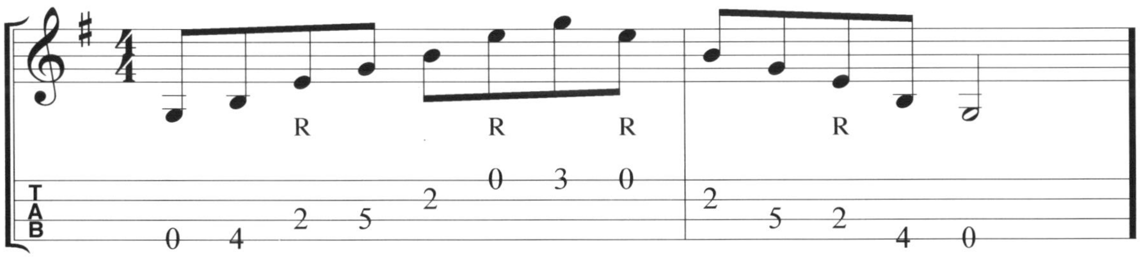

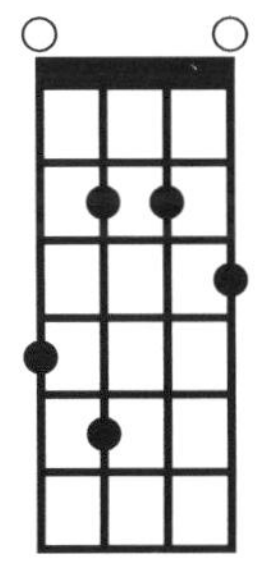

Am

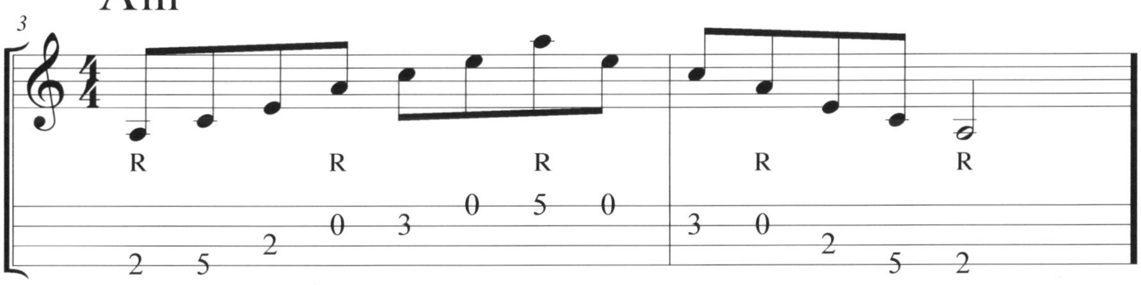

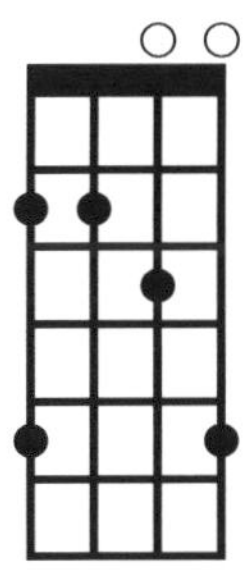

Relative Major/Minor:

Every major chord has a minor counterpart and vice versa. These are known as **relative chords**. Relative chords share two notes from their triads. You can find relative minors by looking at the 6th degree of a major scale. For example: The 6th degree of the G major scale is E, so the relative minor of G is Em. Keep this in mind when learning different minor and major chord tones.

Relative Keys and Minor Pentatonic Scales

As with chords, there exist relative major and minor scales which have the same number of flats or sharps in their key signatures. While relative triads share two notes, relative scales share ALL of their notes. Pentatonic scales further eliminate the characteristic halftones that define major and minor to our ears.

Let's take another look at the G and C major pentatonic scales. Because Em is the relative minor to G, and Am is the relative minor to C, we can use the major pentatonic scales we have already learned for the E and A minor pentatonic scales.

The trick here is to think about the scales around the Em and Am triads, not the G and C triads. Practice playing the scales and thinking about the minor chord tones within each scale.

G Major and E Minor Pentatonic Scales

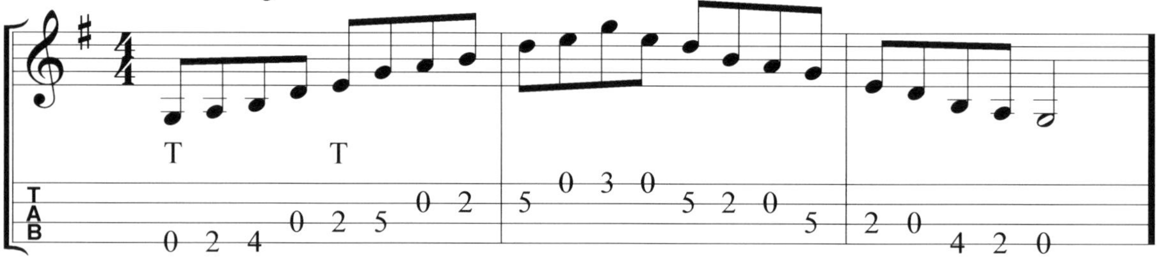

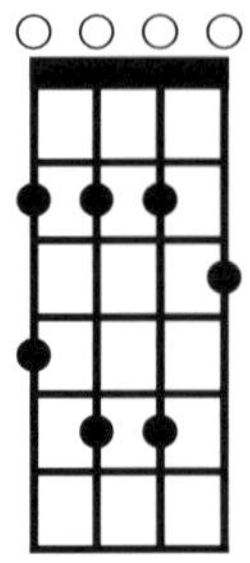

C Major and A Minor Pentatonic Scales

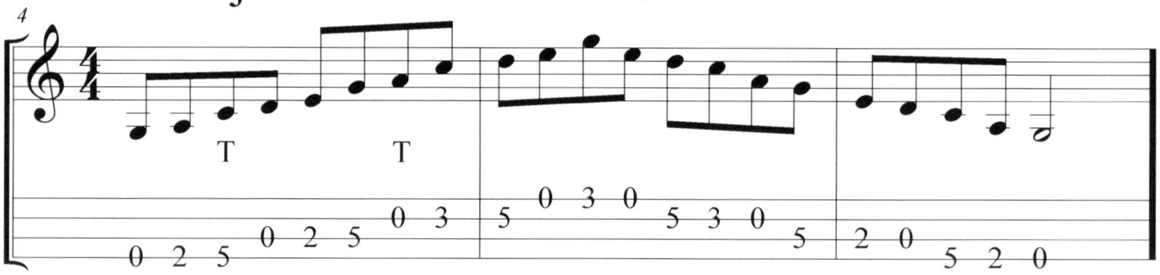

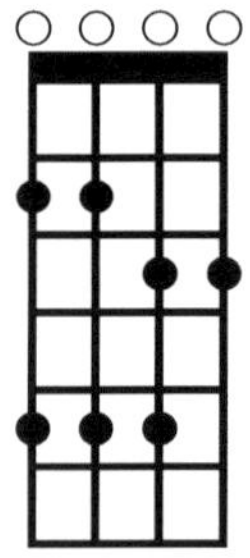

Although they share all the same notes, it helps to think of each relative major and minor scale as two different scales, beginning and ending on different **tonic** or first notes.

Minor Pentatonic Practice Progression

Here is a sample chord progression to help you change between major and minor pentatonic scales.

When changing from G to Em or C to Am, remember to think about chord tones and make a mental note that you are changing scales, even though the notes are the same.

Learn the sample solo below and then write your own:

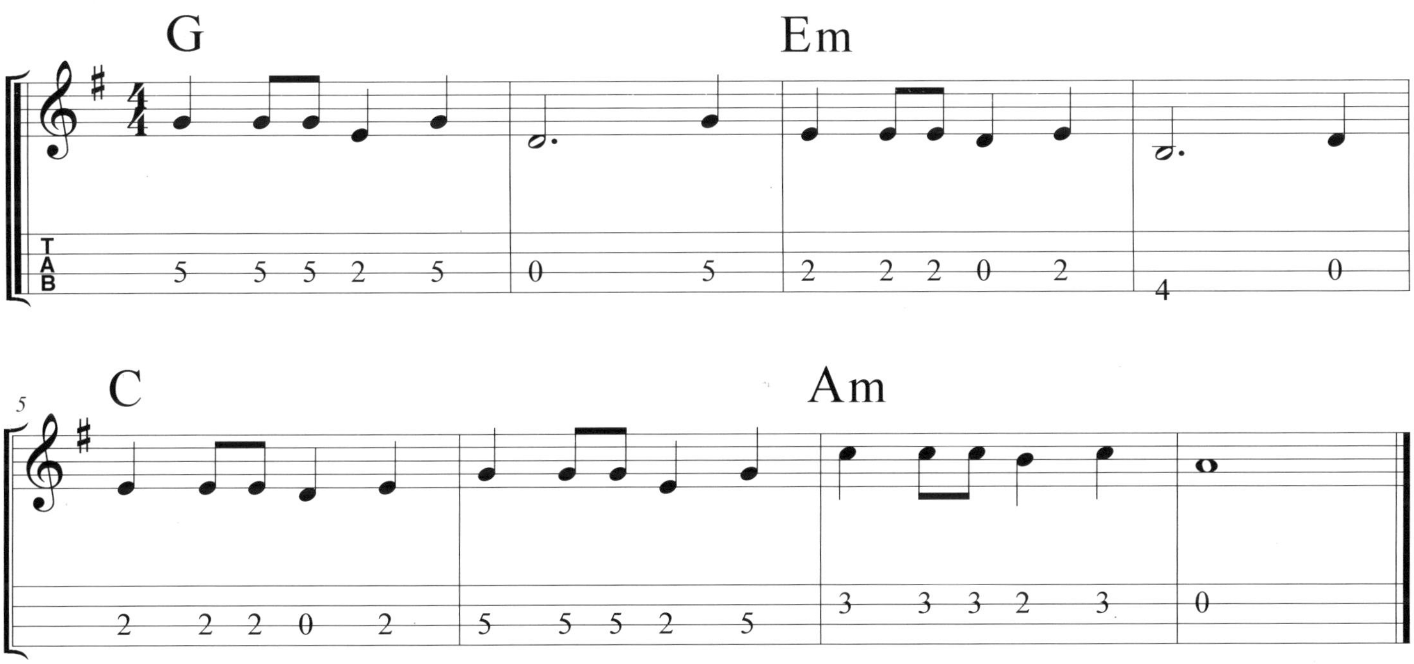

Solo Tip: Melodic Sequencing

In the sample solo above, notice the rhythm that is used at the beginning of every chord change. This is an example of what is called **melodic sequencing**.

A melodic line is presented for the G chord, then slightly altered to fit the Em chord. It is then altered even more to fit the last two chords.

Minor Pentatonic Song Example: "Wayfaring Stranger"

Here is an excerpt from the verse of "Wayfaring Stranger." Just like "Angeline the Baker," this song uses only the pentatonic scale for the melody. Because this song is in a minor key, it uses the Em and Am pentatonic scales.

Learn the melody below and then try to write your own solo using only pentatonic scales. Remember to accent the chord tones when writing your solo!

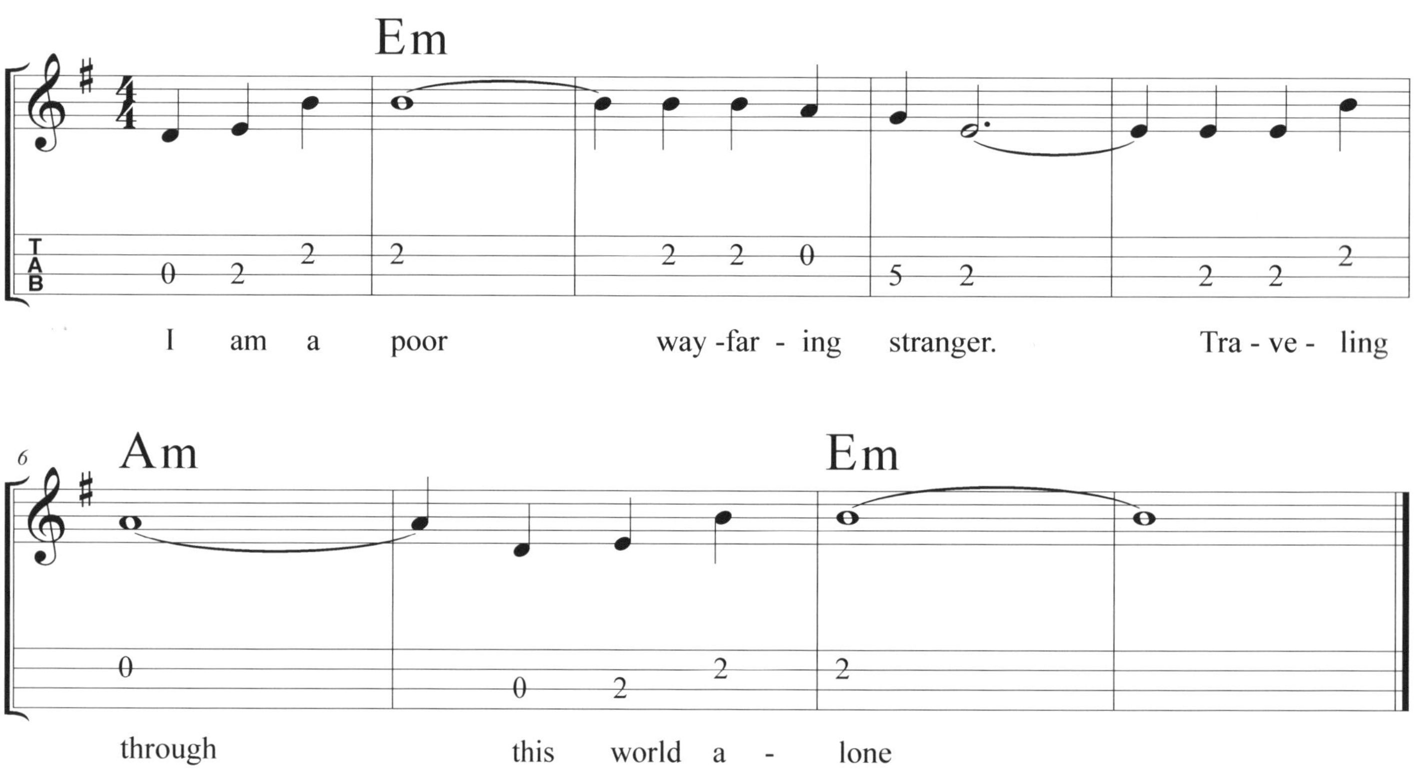

Solo Tip: Less is More!

"Wayfaring Stranger" is a slow, melancholy gospel tune. Notice how the melody is very simple, with long drawn-out notes.

Keep this in mind when writing your own solo to this song. Long notes with a nice mandolin tremolo sound great on this tune!

4. Passing Tones

Passing Tones Between the 2nd and 3rd Scale Degrees

Now that we've learned the major and minor pentatonic scales, it's time to spice them up with some passing tones.

Passing tones are played between scale degrees and, as the name suggests, are meant to be played in a brief temporal fashion. This means that you always go up or down to the next note of the scale after playing a passing tone. Rarely are passing tones held for a long time without going to the next scale degree.

The first passing tone we will learn is between the second and third scale degree of the pentatonic scale. This passing tone is often used in bluegrass and blues, but can be applied to almost any style. Take note of the alternate fingerings in parentheses on the G and D scales. For notes not marked with alternate fingerings, use normal fingerings.

G

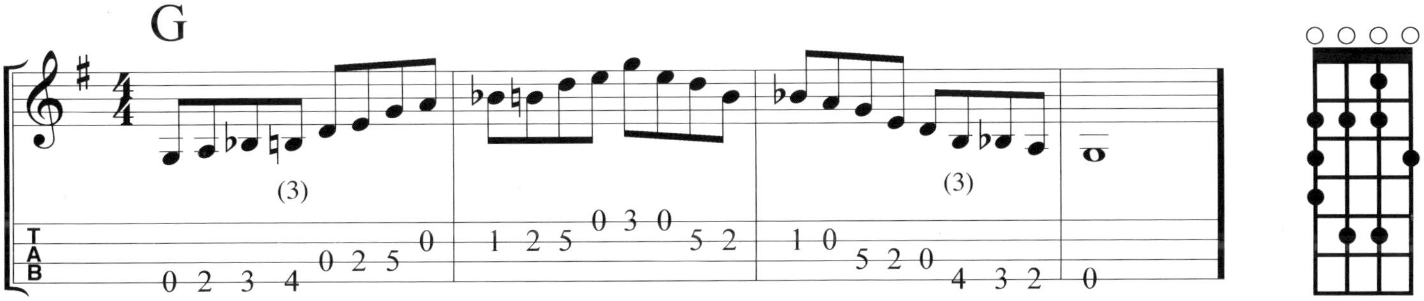

C

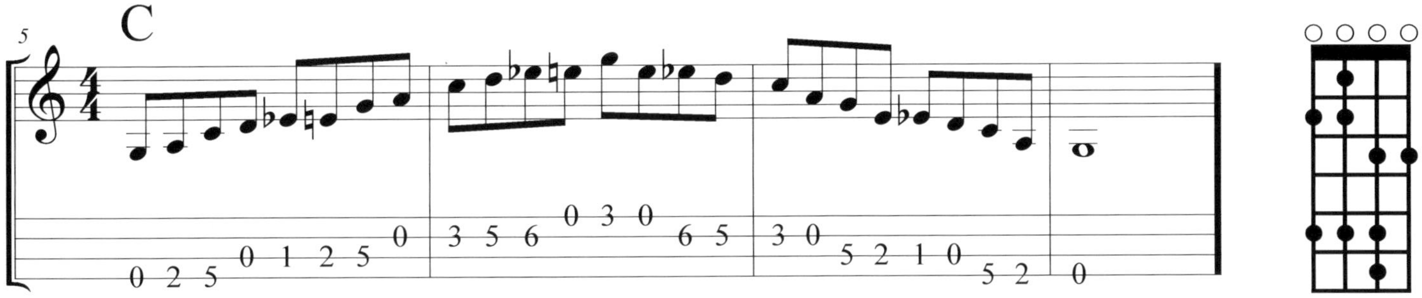

D

Passing Tones Between the 3rd and 5th Scale Degrees

The second set of passing tones comes after the 3rd note of the pentatonic scale. This set actually adds two notes, but only one is considered a passing tone, as the other occurs naturally in the major scale.

Notice that the D scale at the bottom of this page has more total notes than the other two. This is because the passing tones occur over the course of 3 octaves for D, and just two octaves for G and C.

G

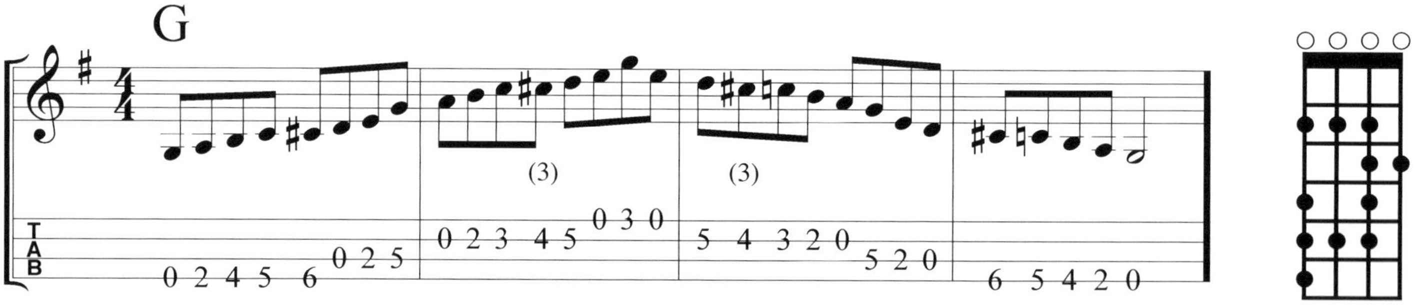

C

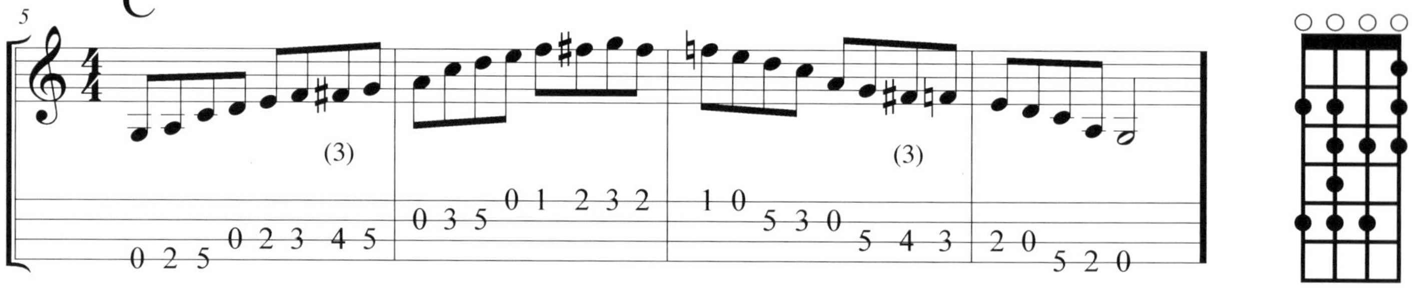

D

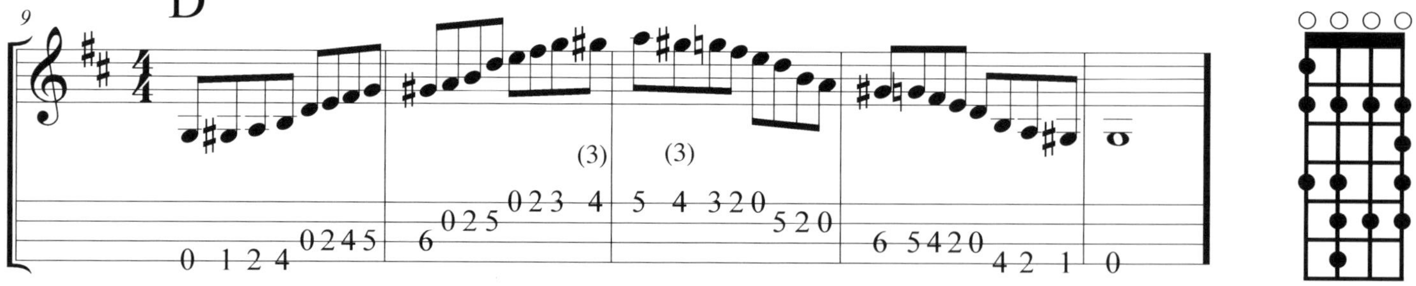

Passing Tone Practice Progression

The solo example below uses the two different passing tones learned in this chapter. Take note of how these passing tones are used, and learn the solo below. When comfortable, write your own solo.

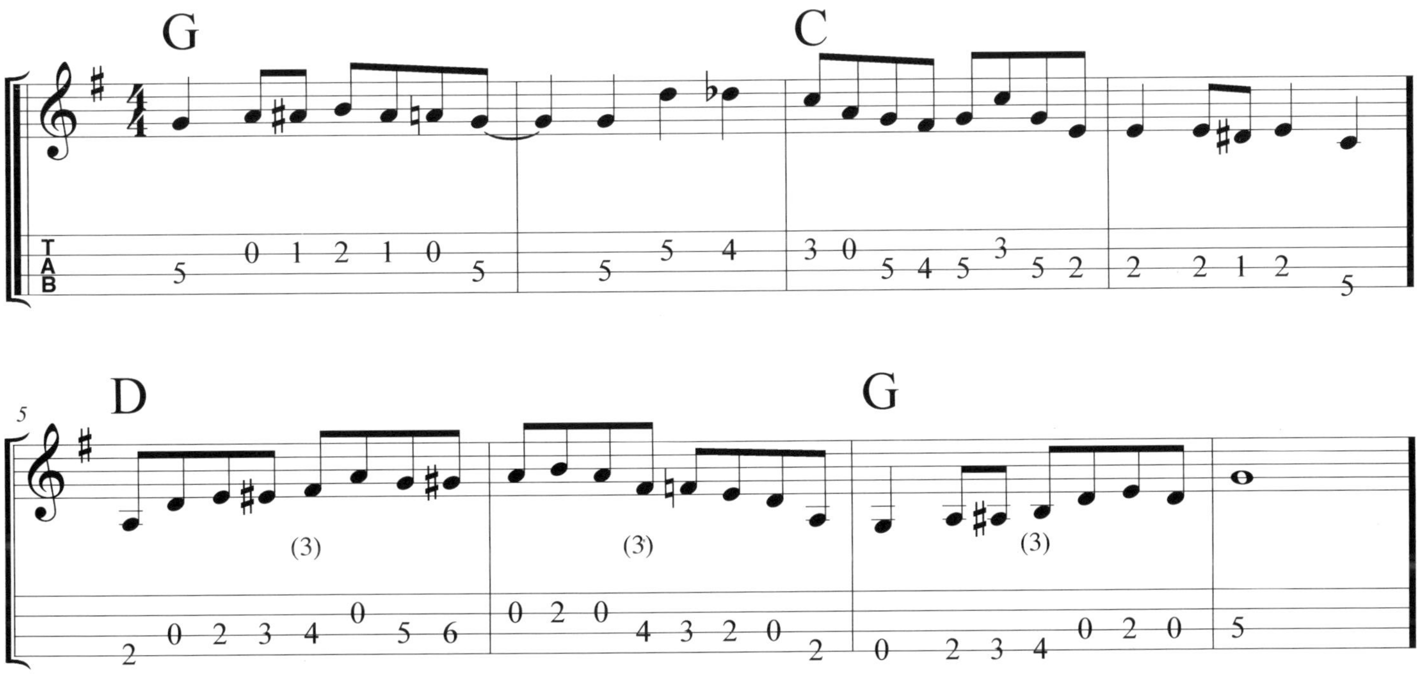

Solo Tip: Use Passing Tones in Passing

Notice in the sample solo above, passing tones are always used to lead to the chord tones surrounding them, and often lead into a chord change. This is a good basic strategy to use when writing or improvising solos.

Licks

Does the phrase in the last two measures of the "Practice Progression" sound familiar? This is a common bluegrass lick. Using licks can spice up and stylize your solos. Later in this chapter we will look at more examples of common licks.

The Minor Pentatonic Blues Scales

Passing tones can also be used in minor scales. Just like major and minor pentatonic scales, these scales use the same notes as their relative major counterparts, as we learned at the beginning of this chapter, "Passing Tones Between the 2nd and 3rd Degrees."

When adding passing tones to the minor pentatonic scale, we create what is known as the **minor pentatonic blues scale**, or simply the "Blues Scale." This scale is widely used in popular music, especially in rock, blues and R&B.

Here are the E minor and A minor pentatonic blues scales:

E Minor Pentatonic Blues Scale

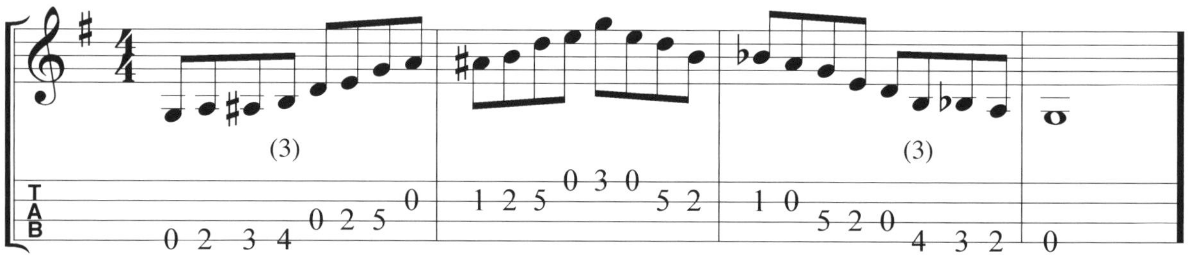

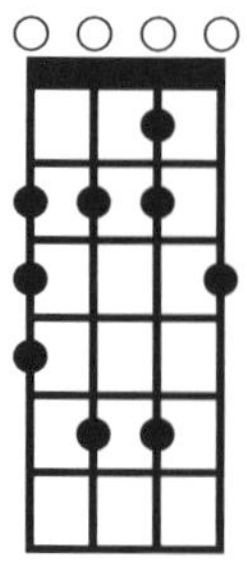

A Minor Pentatonic Blues Scale

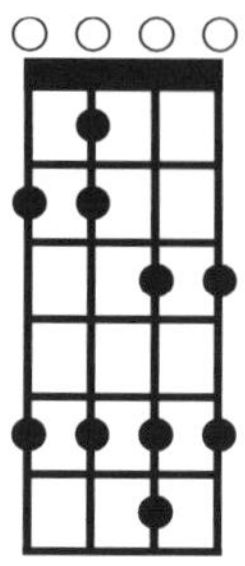

Although they share all the same notes, remember to think of the relative major and minor passing tone scales as two different scales.

Minor Pentatonic Blues Practice Progression

Here is a progression to help practice the different minor blues scales. There is a C chord in this progression to help you change between minor and major passing tone scales.

Learn the sample solo below and then write your own:

Solo Tip: Theme and Variation

When improvising, try to establish a **theme** that repeats throughout the solo. In the solo above, a theme is presented in the first two measures, then altered twice in the next four measures. Finally, the theme is repeated without alteration in the last two measures.

The G Run and Other Licks

Here are some common licks and phrases used in bluegrass and other styles. Learning licks can help your playing sound more authentic and "in the style" of the genre. It is a good idea to study other players' solos and licks to improve your phrasing.

The first lick below is the common bluegrass "G run", named because it is commonly played with a G chord on guitar. This lick uses the first passing tone that we learned at the beginning of the chapter. It is listed below for the G, C and D chords.

Note: The G run for the G chord can be played in two octaves in open position on the mandolin, and is shown below.

Other Licks

Bluegrass Walkup

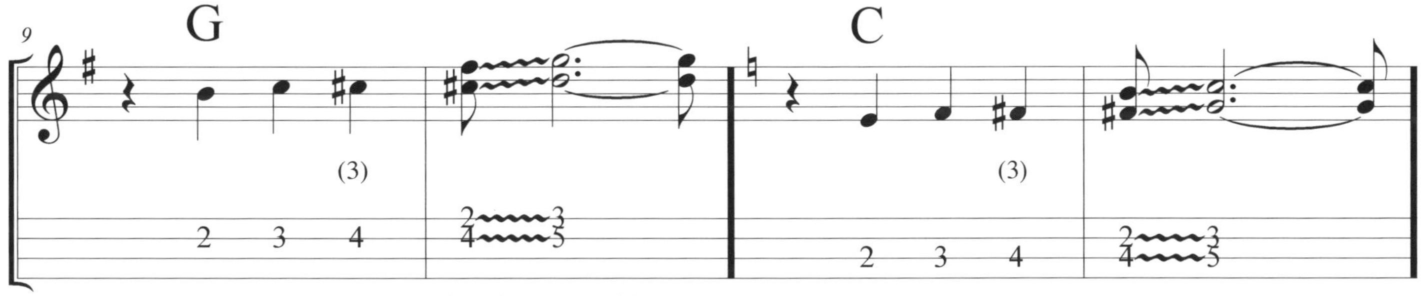

The above marking denotes a slide.

Banjo Fill

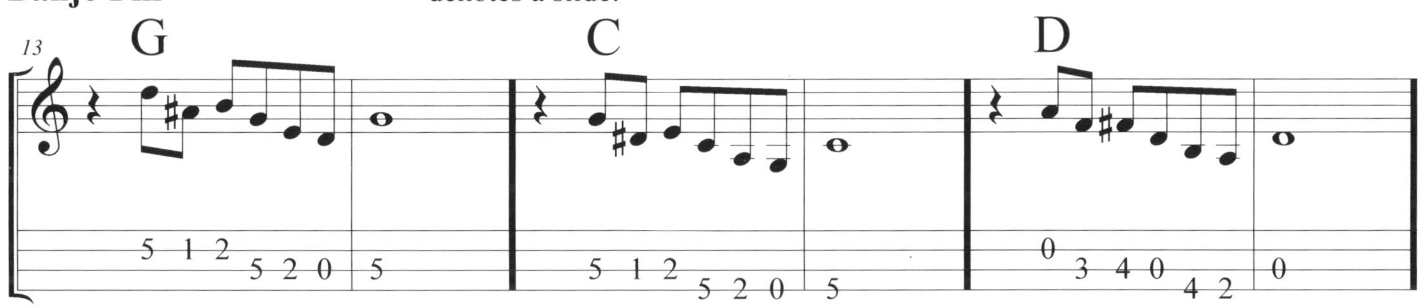

Minor Bluegrass Run

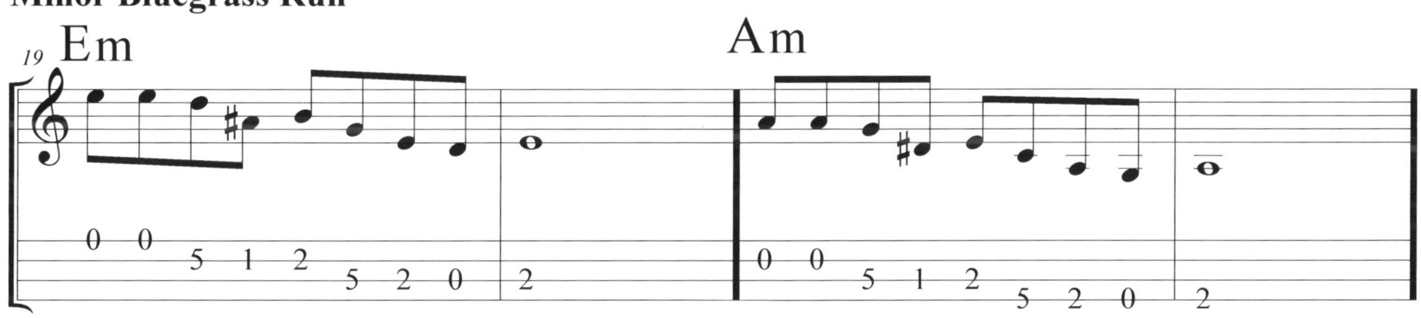

Jazz Turnaround

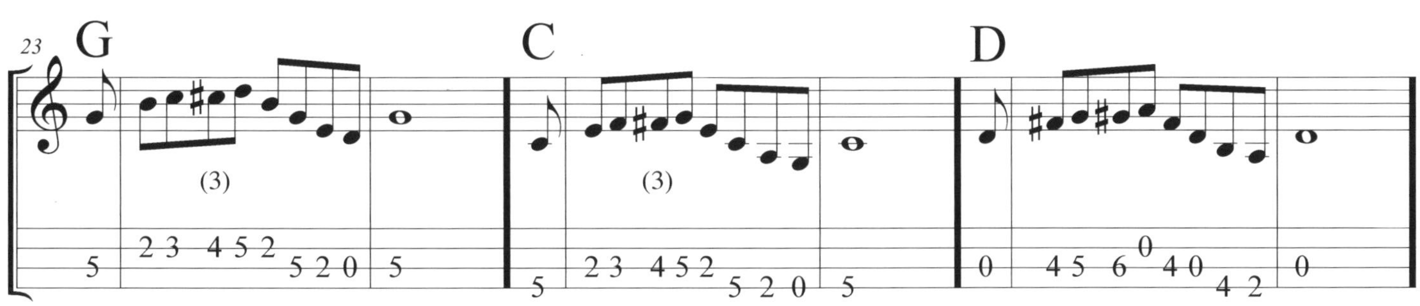

Jazz Minor Turnaround

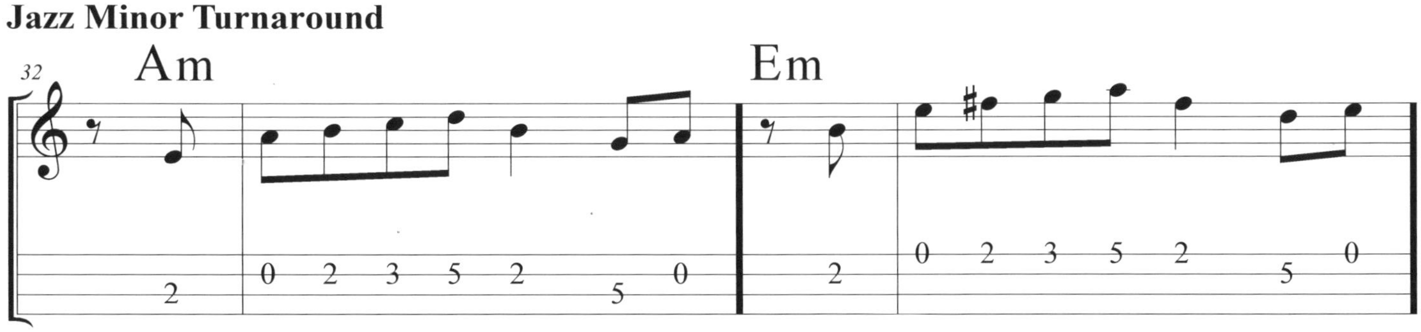

Passing-Tone Song Example: "Billy in the Lowground"

Here is the A section of the popular fiddle tune, "Billy in the Lowground." This song mixes minor and major chords and serves as a good example for switching passing-tone scales. It even features some passing tones in the melody.

Pay attention to the scale tones in the melody and notice the interchange of passing tones, pentatonic scales, and triads.

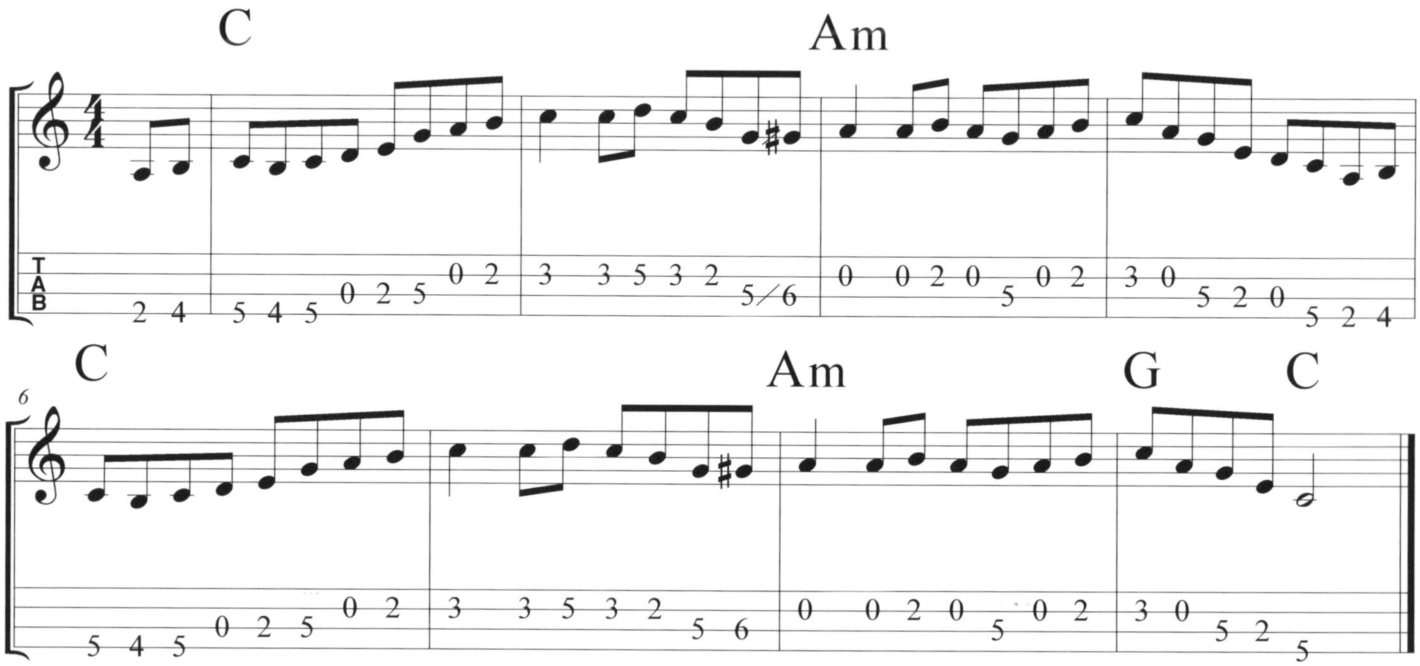

Major Scale:

"Billy in the Lowground" is unique in its use of a mixture of major, pentatonic, and pentatonic passing-tone scales. The 4th note in the song is a B, which is in the C major scale, but not in the triad, pentatonic, or blues scales that we have learned. We haven't discussed incorporating the major scale, but this is a good example of throwing in a note from it while still sticking mostly to pentatonic scales and passing tones. See if you can pick out where the melody uses each scale.

Quick Chord Changes

The G chord near the end of this song goes by pretty quickly, and you might have noticed that the melody does not even change to a G scale of any kind. Because the chord change is so fast, you can get by without changing scales for it, although changing scales would be fine.

5. Adding the Dominant 7th

You might have seen chords in certain songs such as G7 or C7. These chords are known as **dominant 7ths** and naturally occur as the **V** chord in the major scale.

Dominant 7th chords are major triads with an added "7th" note on top of the 5th. These 4-note chords have a tense sound to them and sound nice when played right before a **I** chord.

Let's begin by looking back at our original triads and adding the 7th note. Memorize these chord tones and think about their natural key. Note that G7 would occur naturally in the key of C; that's why the F is natural rather than F♯.

G7 (V)

C7 (V)

D7 (V)

The Dominant 7th Pentatonic Scale

To make use of dominant 7th notes in solos, all you need to do is add them to the scales we have already learned. Take note of where each 7th note lands for each chord, and add that note to the major pentatonic scale.

Below are examples of major pentatonic scales with the added 7th note. Remember, you can also add these 7th notes to the passing-tone scales from the previous chapter.

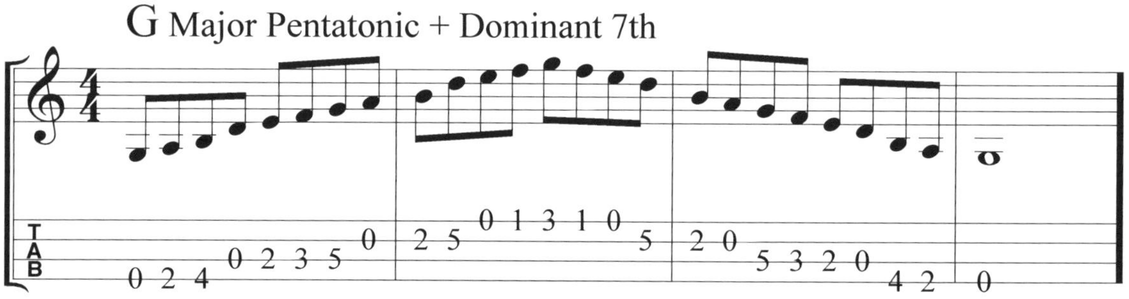

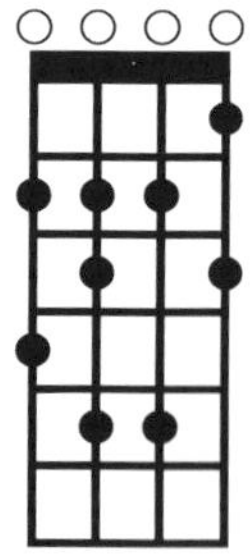

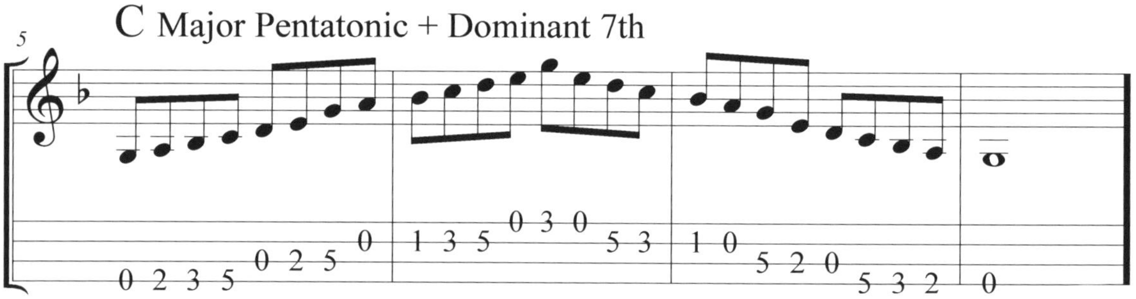

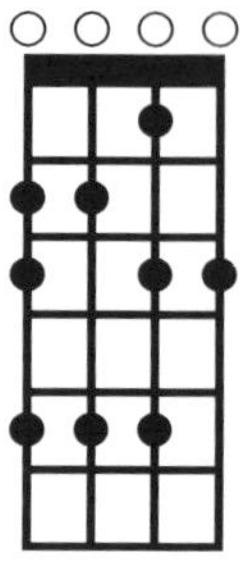

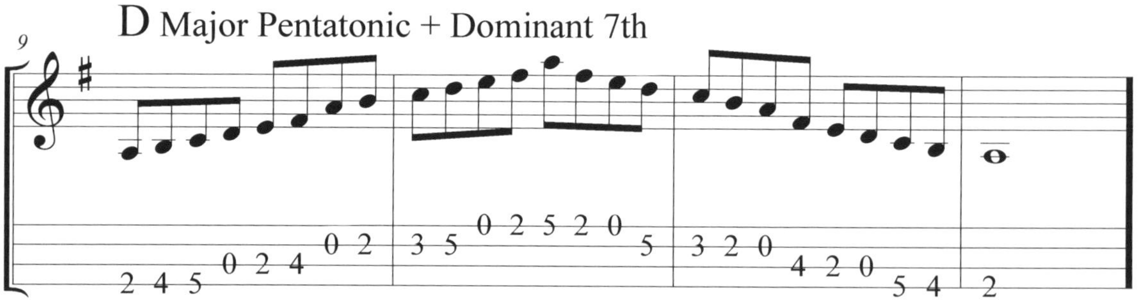

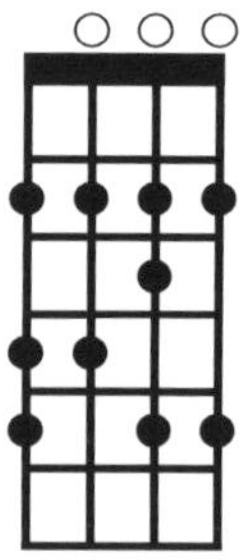

Dominant 7th Uses and Practice Progression

Adding the 7th to your solos can make them sound cool and interesting, but adding it over the wrong chords can sound like a mistake.

As mentioned earlier, the **V** chord is naturally a dominant chord, so you are ok to use the 7th anytime a **V** chord appears.

A good starting point for now is to save the 7ths for 7th chords. Here is a sample solo that mixes use of the pentatonic scales, passing tones, and 7ths. Learn the solo and pay attention to where it uses 7th notes. After learning the solo, write your own.

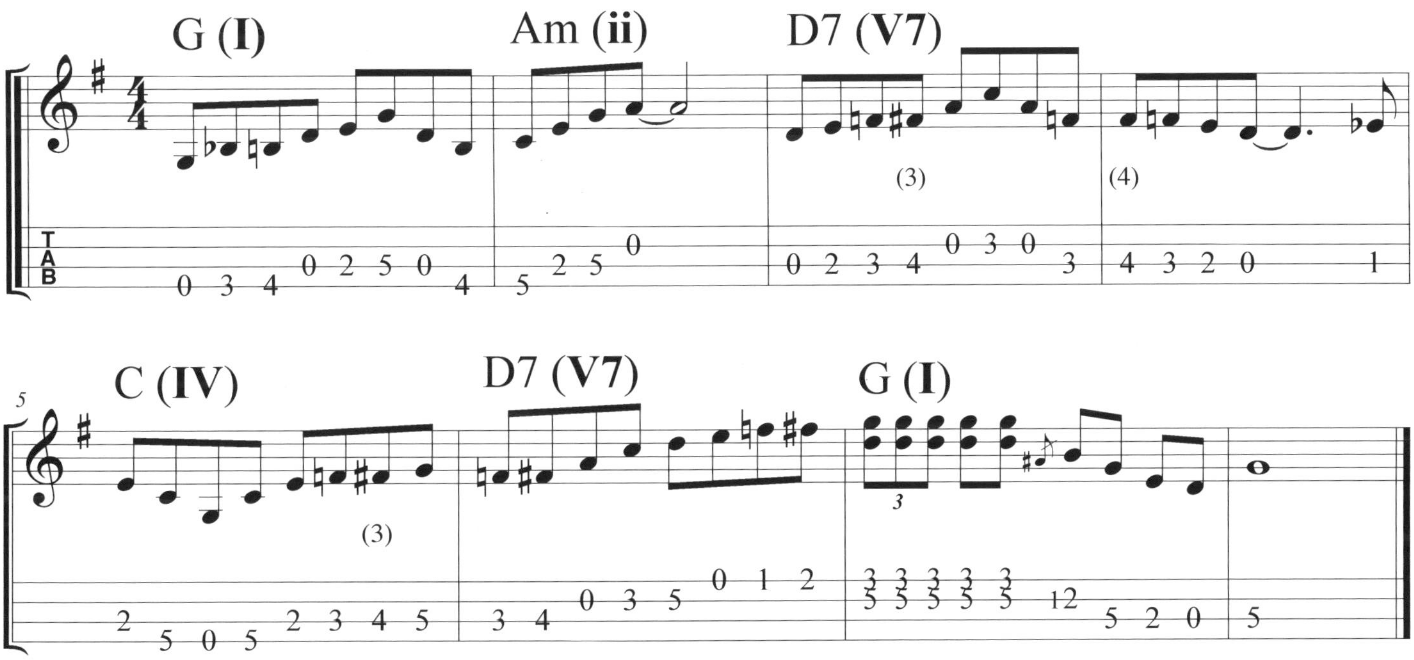

Solo Tip: Leading Tones

Notice how the solo above uses passing tones and other scale notes to lead from one chord to another. This technique, known as **lead-tone soloing**, is widely used in improvisation. When you're coming close to a chord change, think about where the closest chord tone of the next chord is and try to land on it using a passing tone or just a normal scale note.

The Blues

Learning 7ths is a great time to learn how to play the blues.

A blues progression takes a normal chord progression using **I, IV, and V** and makes not just the **V** chord a 7th chord, but ALL of the chords 7ths:

I7 - IV7 - V7

Blues progressions are a great way to practice 7th chords, and are very common in bluegrass, jazz and of course, blues. Being able to play a good blues solo is imperative to modern improvisation.

Here is the blues progression with a sample solo for you to practice. Learn the solo and practice improvising your own. Try to hit the 7th notes on every chord.

Minor Pentatonic Blues Scale Revisited

When listening to the sample solo over the blues progression, you might have noticed that the solos didn't sound quite as dark or bluesy as some of the blues solos you are used to hearing. This is because a lot of musicians choose to play a different scale over the blues progression: The minor pentatonic blues scale, AKA, the **blues scale**!

Although the blues scale is based around minor chords, when played over their major counterparts (ex. G minor pentatonic blues over G major), they create a completely different sound.

Here is a sample solo using just the G blues scale. Because the G blues scale doesn't feature every chord tone for each chord, this solo focuses on landing on the few chord tones that do occur.

Solo Tip: The Blue Note

The blues scale sounds great over the blues progression because of the clash of the minor 3rd in the scale with the major 3rd in the chord. This clash gives a sense of a note in between the two, known as the **blue note**. Giving a slight bend to the string when playing the minor 3rd (B♭ in the progression above) will create the blue note itself. Experiment with this note to give your solos a bluesier sound.

6. The Major Scale

Major scales contain every note in a key, and therefore contain all the chord tones for every chord in that key. Knowing the major scale can help give you a safety net in your soloing if you get lost changing chords.

When soloing, I tend to focus on chord tones and pentatonic scales first, rather than the major scale. From my personal experience, it's harder to make your solos sound musical without first learning how to play to each chord within a progression.

Thinking about changing chord tones and pentatonic scales on each chord may be harder than just using one scale for a song, but it will make your solos sound more musical. It will also help prepare you for more complex songs and progressions.

Learn each scale below and remember, each scale represents a **key**, not a chord. If a song is in the key of C, play the C major scale over all the chords.

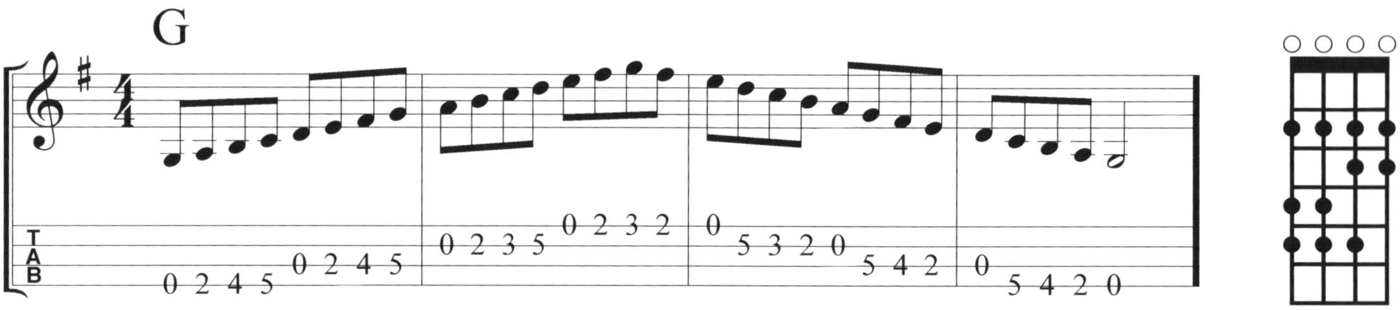

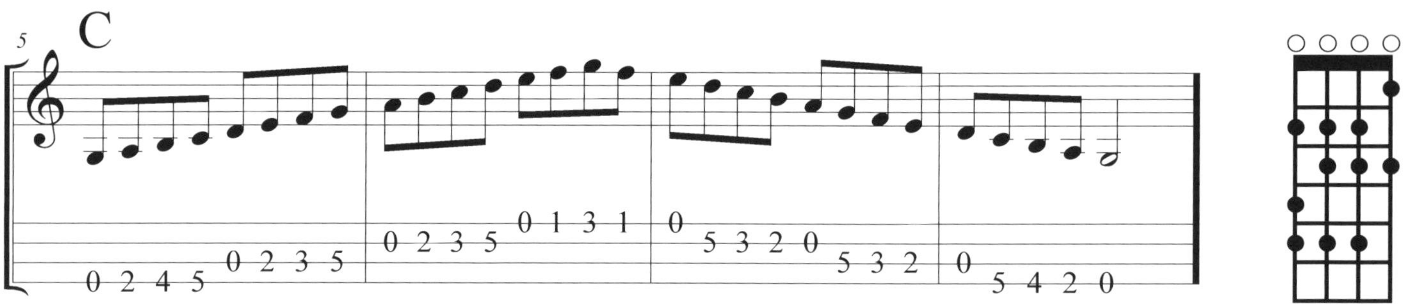

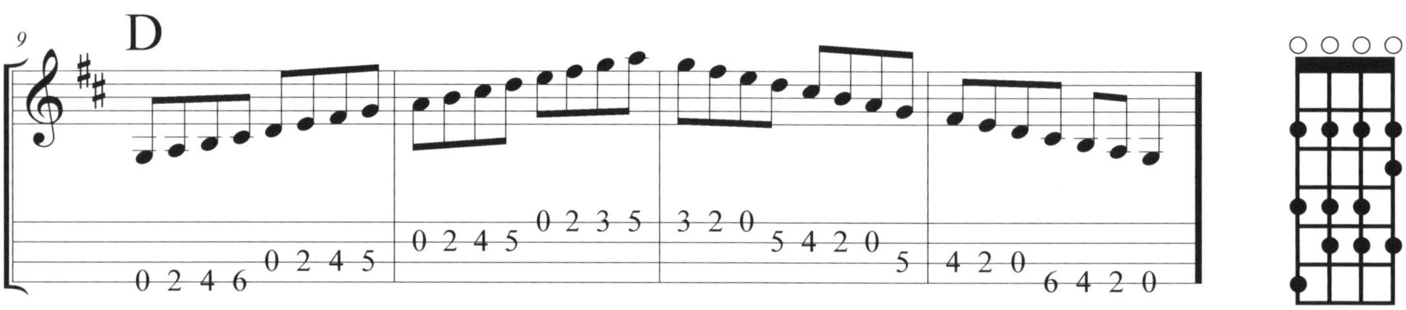

When Not to Use the Major Scale

In some instances, the major scale will not work over every chord in a key. For example, in the key of C major, if you play the G major scale over the $\mathbf{V}^7$ (G) chord, the F♯ will clash with the F natural of the chord. In this instance, the F♯ could only be played as a passing tone.

The Blues

When soloing over a blues progression, playing a major scale over each of the chords will not work. This is because all of the chords in a blues progression are dominant 7th chords. The major scale only works when every chord **naturally occurs** in the major key. The **I** chord in the major scale is not naturally a dominant chord, so when a blues progression changes it to dominant, the major scale no longer works.

Minor Keys

This one is obvious. For minor keys, minor scales are used.

Songs with Key Changes

Many songs change keys in the middle of the song. Jazz tunes often change keys every few chords! In these types of complex songs, it is better to focus on playing around the chords because in many cases, there won't be a specific scale that fits every chord.

There are many more examples of when **not** to use the major scale. The best way to figure out whether the major scale works over a progression is to study the melody and analyze the chords. Also, use your ear! A lot of times you can hear which notes will work and which will not.

Major Scale Song Example: "Blackberry Blossom"

Here is the A section of the fiddle tune "Blackberry Blossom." This tune uses the major scale for most of the melody, and is also a great left-hand exercise.

Learn the melody slowly before trying to play it at a faster speed.

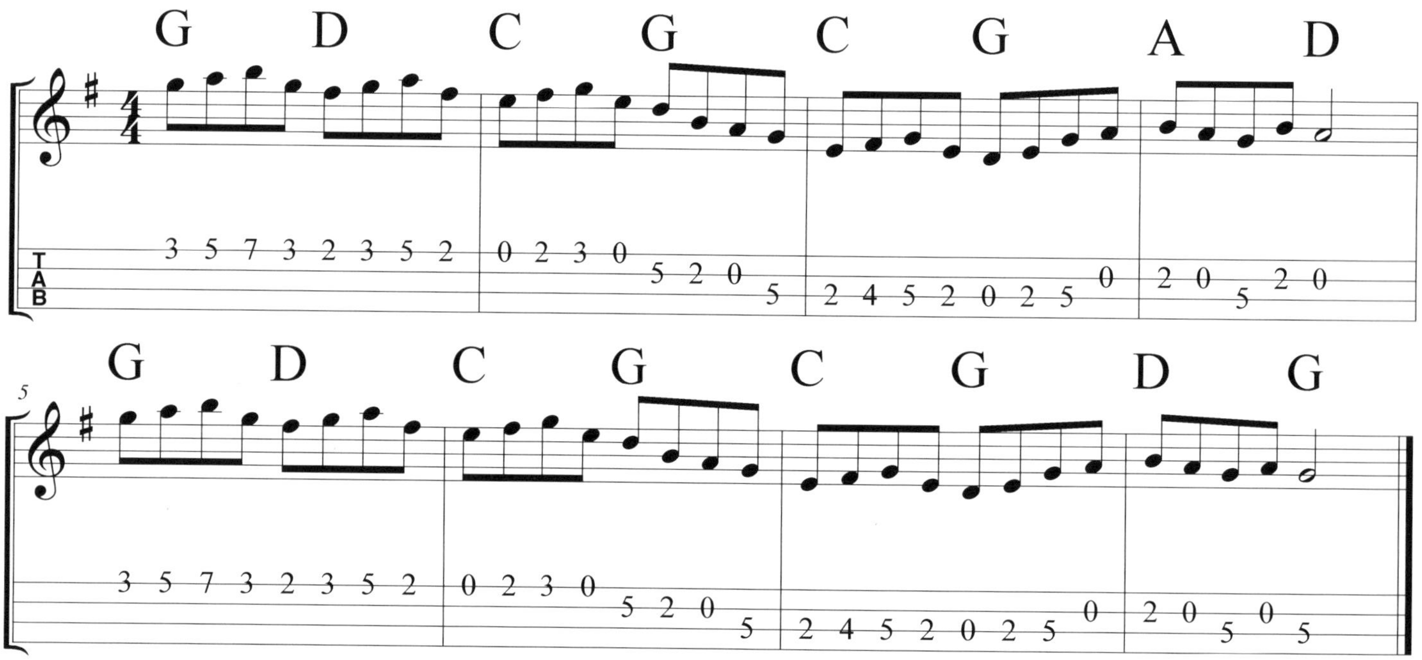

Quick Chord Changes Revisited

The entire A section of "Blackberry Blossom" has fast chord changes. This is where the major scale comes into play. It is challenging to focus on playing the different pentatonic scales for each chord, and would most likely produce a mechanical sounding solo. Since the G major scale fits over each chord (other than the A chord), it's much easier and more efficient to solo using the major scale.

Notice that although the melody uses the major scale, it still plays around the tones of each chord. Remember to take note of the chord tones being played as you learn the melody.

Major Scale Practice Progression

"The Major Scale Practice Progression" uses the exact progression from the song example, "Blackberry Blossom." These chord changes provide a complex palette with many different improvisational possibilities. The sample solo below uses predominately the major scale, but also throws in passing tones and pentatonic scales.

Learn the solo below, then write your own:

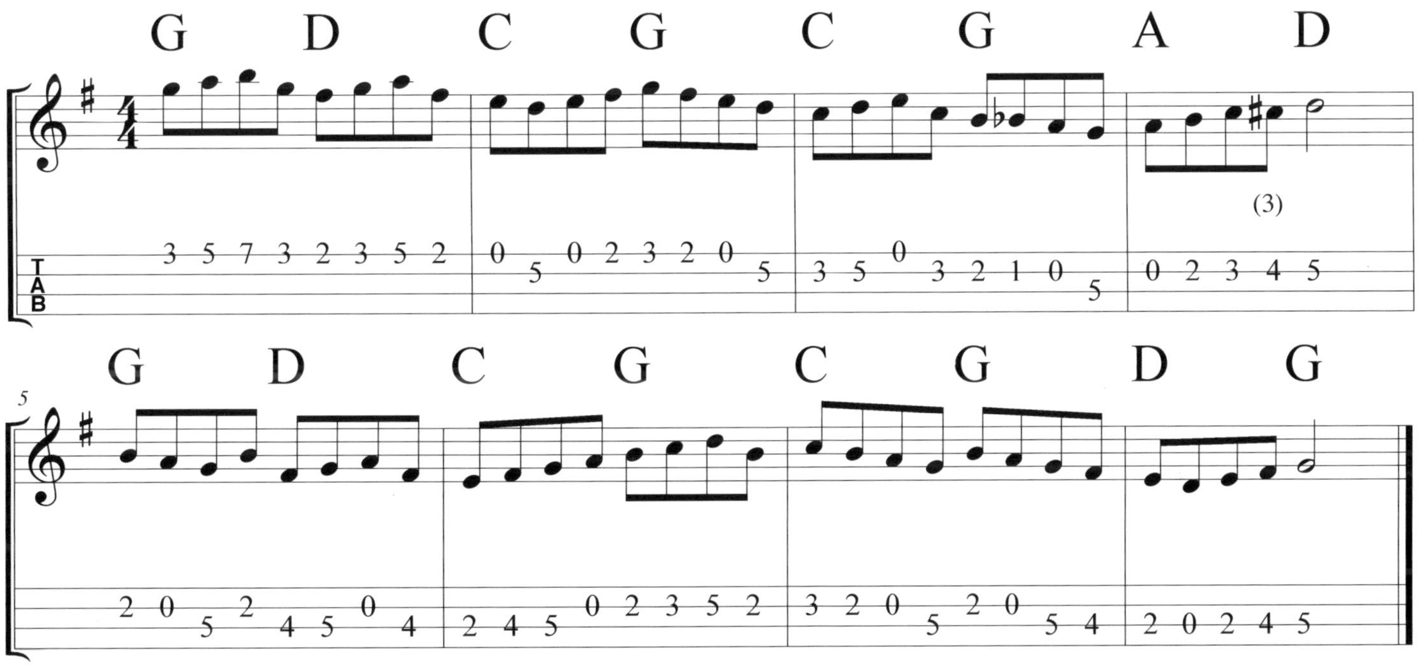

Solo Tip: Embellishing the Melody

The first few measures of this sample solo take the melody from "Blackberry Blossom" and alter it. This is an example of embellishing the original melody of the song during a solo. When having trouble improvising a solo to a song, take the melody and alter the notes or rhythm to make it your own. This will give you a starting point and new ideas as you continue to develop your own solo. This technique is the root of improvisation.

7. The Minor Scale

Just like the major scale in major keys, the minor scale can be used over songs in minor keys. There are three different types of minor scales, but for this chapter we are looking at what is known as the **pure** or **natural minor scale**. Just like pentatonic scales, each minor scale has a relative major scale. For example, the notes of the G major scale and E minor scale are the same.

When learning these, keep in mind where the tonic notes are and try to hear them at the beginning of the scale. Practice each scale starting on the tonic note as well.

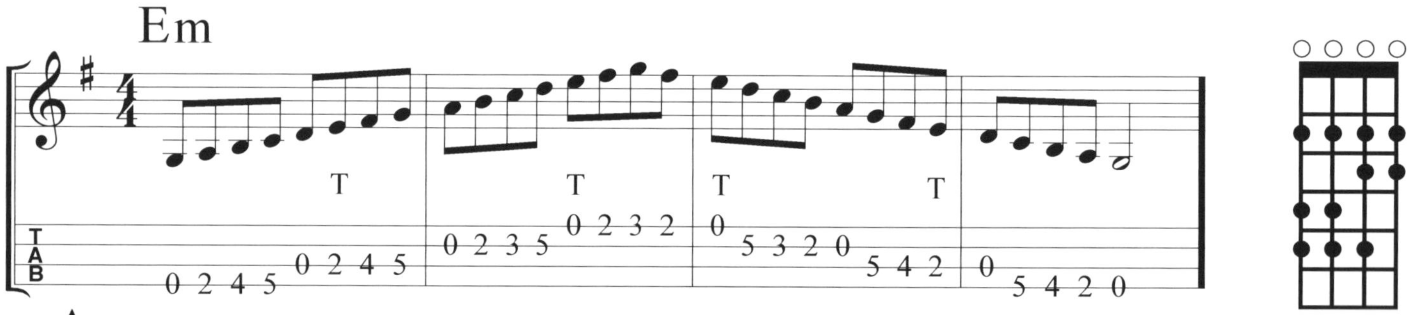

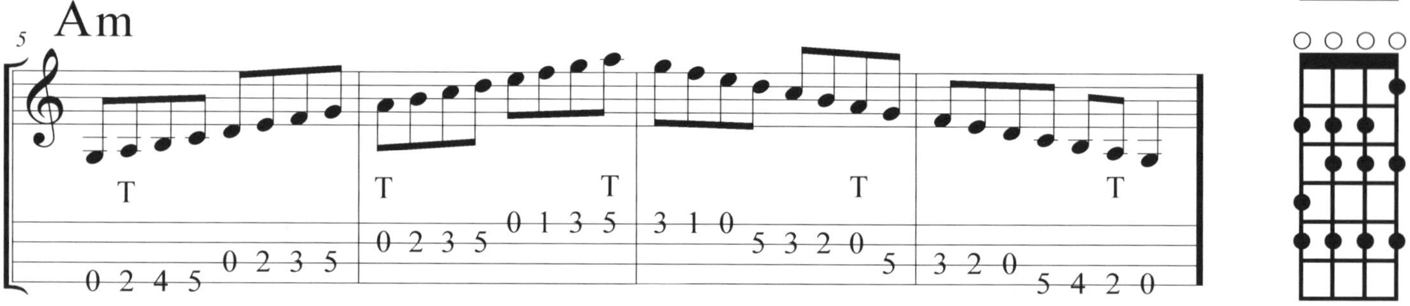

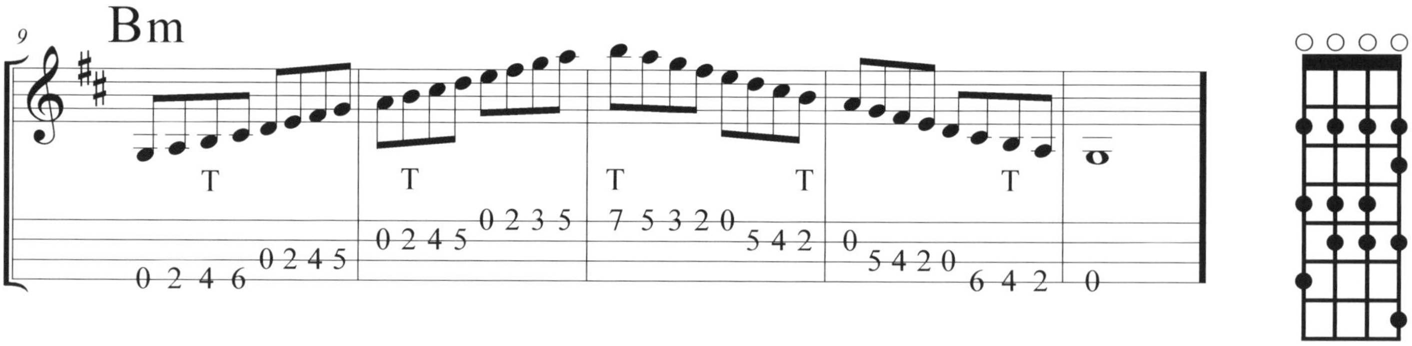

When to Use the Natural Minor Scale

Because there are three types of minor scales, finding where to use the natural minor scale can be a bit tricky. When analyzing the chords of a song in a minor key, check to see whether all the chords naturally fit into the key. This technique, along with following the melody and using your ear, is a great way to determine whether you can use the natural minor scale for the whole song.

Minor Scale Practice Progression

The following "Practice Progression" uses only minor chords. For the solo that is written, the E natural minor scale is used along with the E minor pentatonic blues scale. Pay attention to where passing tones are used, and where chord tones are outlined.

Learn the solo below, then write your own:

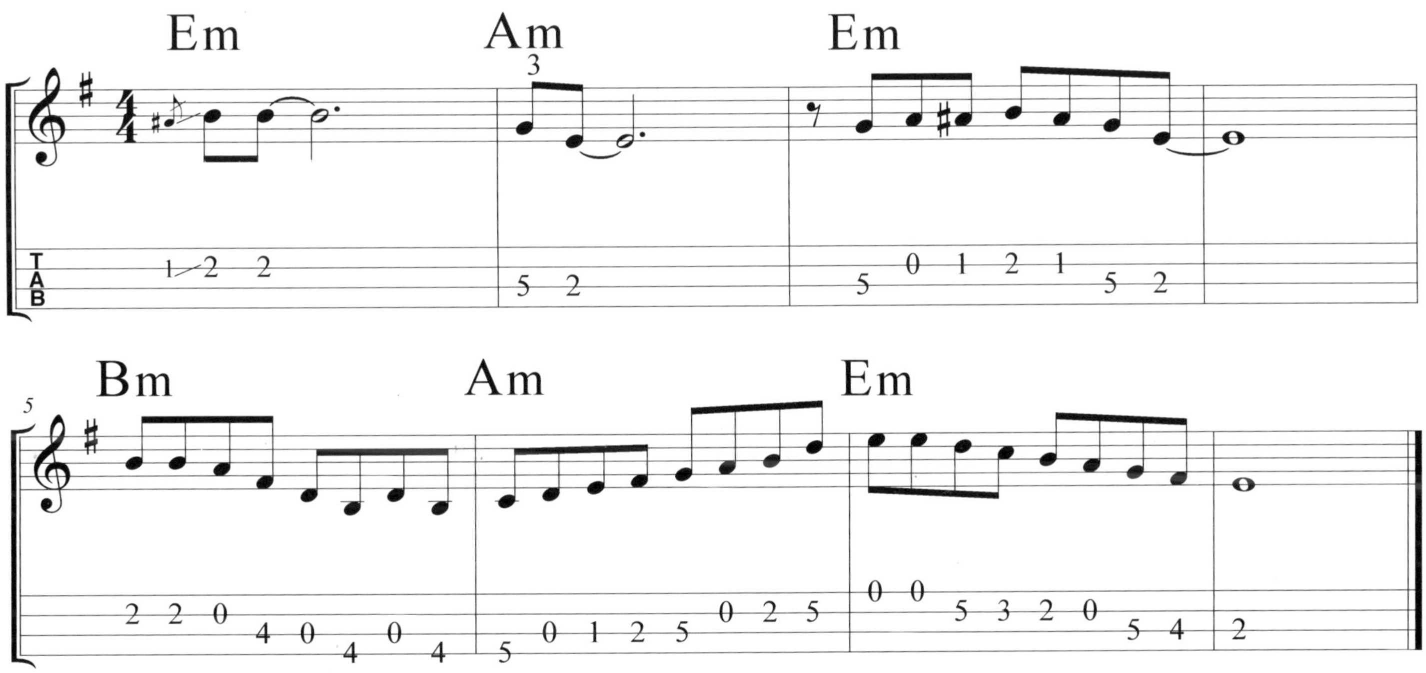

Solo Tip: Rhythmic Variation

Since this chord progression uses only minor chords, it lends itself to a more serious tone. This gives you the ability to make your solo sound more dramatic.

One way to accomplish this is through rhythmic variation. The sample solo above starts out with just a few notes being played, which gives it a somber feeling. During the Bm chord, the solo picks up and uses faster rhythms to make the solo sound more exciting. Finally, for the last two chords, the faster rhythm continues, and builds up to a dramatic finish.

8. Changing Open Keys

Up to this point, every song we have learned has centered around the key of G major or it's relative minor, Em. Chapter 9 will focus on playing in **closed position**, where you can switch to any key. There are a few other keys, however, that work well in open position.

To learn these keys, you just have to use the same method used in the previous chapters. Use the appendix at the end of the book to learn the different arpeggios and scales. There is also a list of play-along practice tracks in different keys in the appendix.

Here is the method you should use to learn new keys:

Let's say we are in the key of A: The three basic major chords in that key are A, D, and E. We have already learned our scales for the D chord, so we just have to learn A and E.

Let's start with A:

Step 1: Learn the triad tones for the A chord:

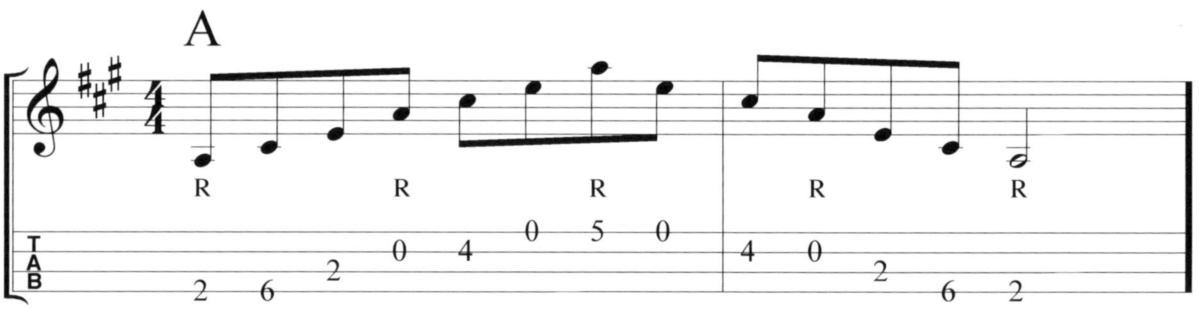

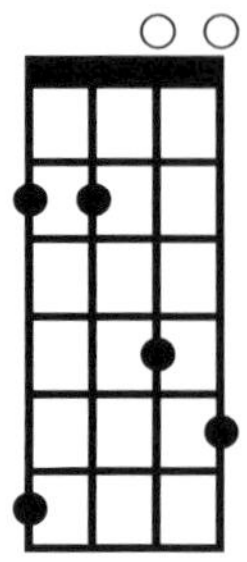

Step 2: Expand the arpeggio to a pentatonic scale:

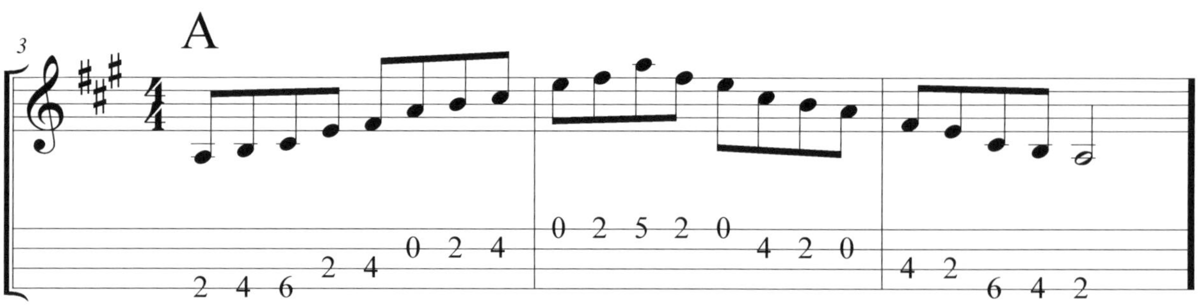

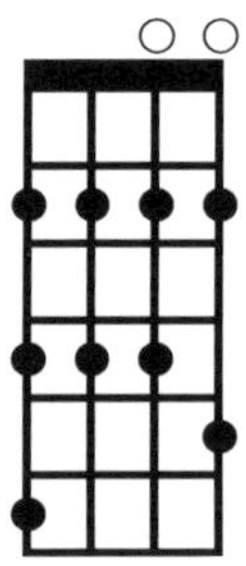

Changing Open Keys Continued

Step 3: Learn the passing tone between the 2nd and 3rd degrees of the scale:

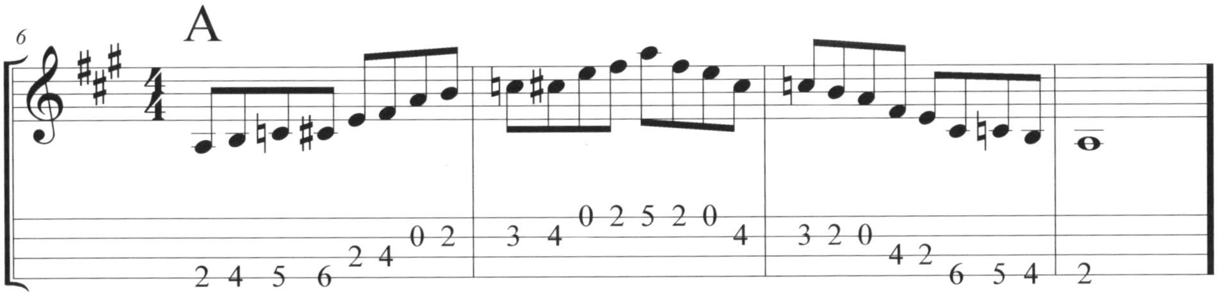

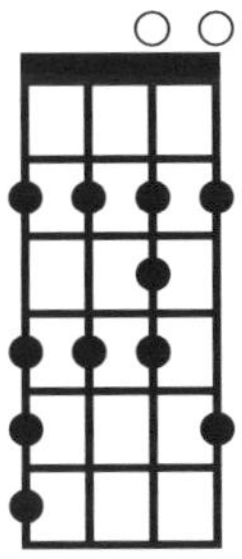

Step 4: Learn the passing tone between the 3rd and 5th notes of the scale:

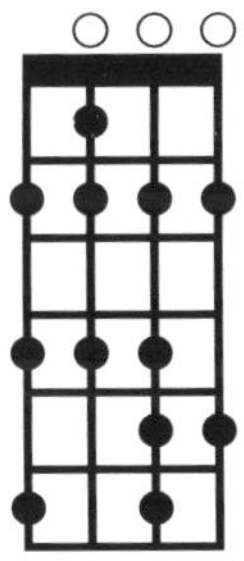

Step 5: Add the dominant 7th:

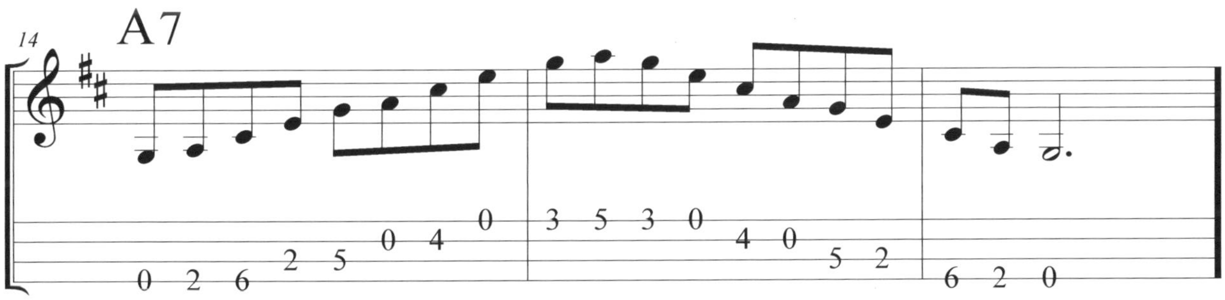

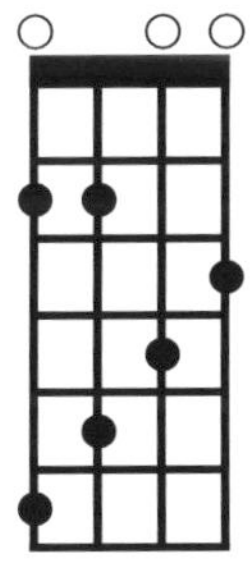

Now we have learned all the variations of an A major chord. The next step would be to repeat steps 1-5 on all the other major chords in the key; in key of **A**; the major chords are E and D.

After that, move to the minor chords: Bm, C♯m, and F♯m. With minor chords the steps are a little simpler:

1. Learn the chord tones.
2. Learn the pentatonic scale.
3. Learn the minor pentatonic blues scale.

Once you've learned all the chords in the key, next learn the major and relative minor scales for the key:

A

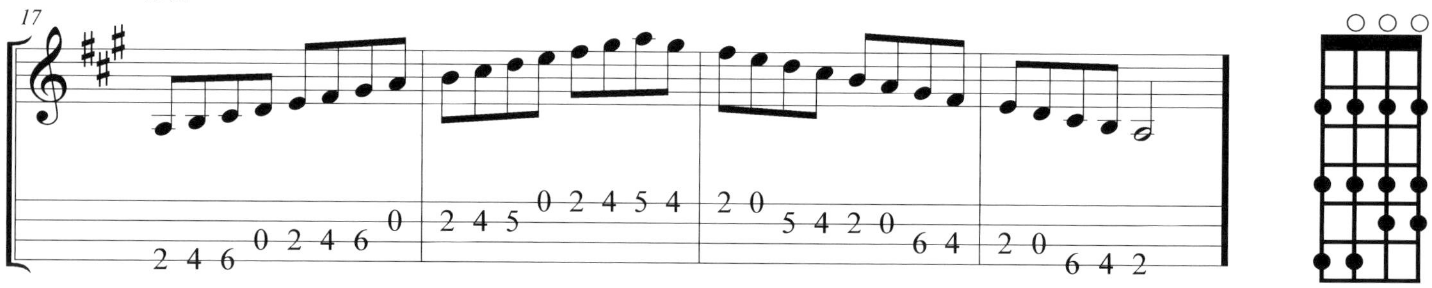

F♯m

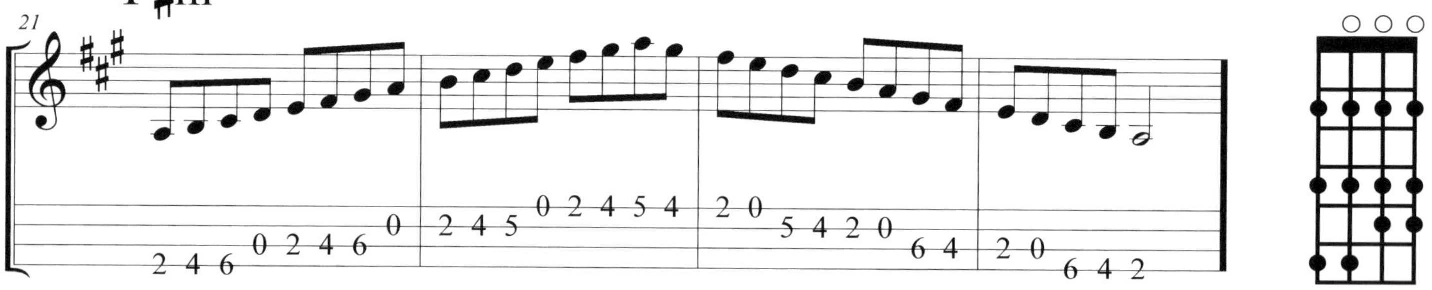

After you have learned the major and minor scales, you have mastered the key!

Keeping in mind that different keys share some of the same chords; here is my recommended order for learning all of the open keys, with the chords of the key listed to the right:

Group 1:

1. G major/E minor (G, C, D, Am, Bm, Em)
2. D major/B minor (D, G, A, Em, F♯m, Bm)
3. A major/F♯ minor (A, D, E, Bm, C♯m, F♯m)
4. E major/C♯ minor (E, A, B, F♯m, G♯m, C♯m)

Group 2:

1. C major/A minor (C, F, G, Dm, Em, Am)
2. F major/D minor (F, B♭, C, Gm, Am, Dm)
3. B♭ major/G minor (B♭, E♭, F, Cm, Dm, Gm)
4. E♭ major/C minor (E♭, A♭, B♭, Fm, Gm, Cm)

Although this seems like a lot of work, if you learn the keys in that order, you only have to learn one major and one minor chord for each new key.

9. Closed Position and Moving Up the Neck

Up to this point, we have only discussed chord tones and scales in open position. This is where the majority of your soloing will take place, but it is good to be able to solo anywhere on the mandolin and utilize notes in the higher register.

Once you move up the neck in **closed position**, you only have to learn one pattern per scale or arpeggio, and you can move the pattern up or down the fretboard.

Scale Boxes

The best way to learn how to play in closed position is to learn two different one-octave areas, which I call **scale boxes**. These boxes start with a note, and move to the next octave of the note. I like to call these outside notes the **handles**. You change chord arpeggios and scales by changing the notes in between the handles of the scale box. Pay attention to which fingers play each handle. These will stay the same on every scale box. They use similar fingerings as open position scales by playing the lowest numbered fret with your first finger. Here are the two scale boxes with just their handles:

Scale Box 1:

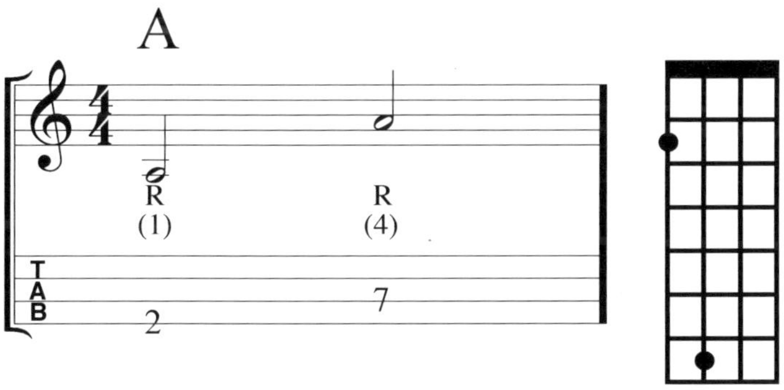

Scale Box 2:

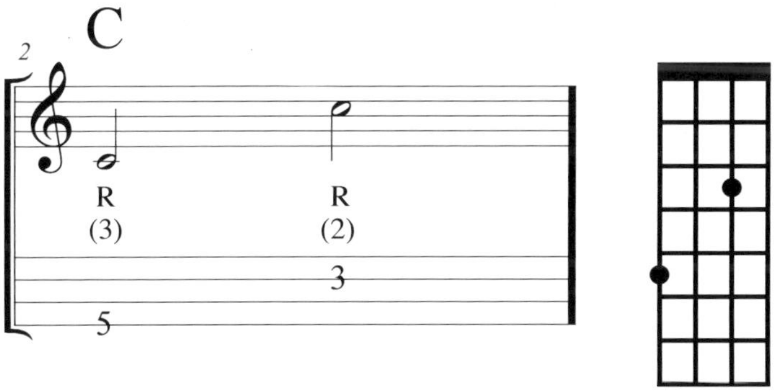

Here is an example of the scale boxes filled-in with a major triad:

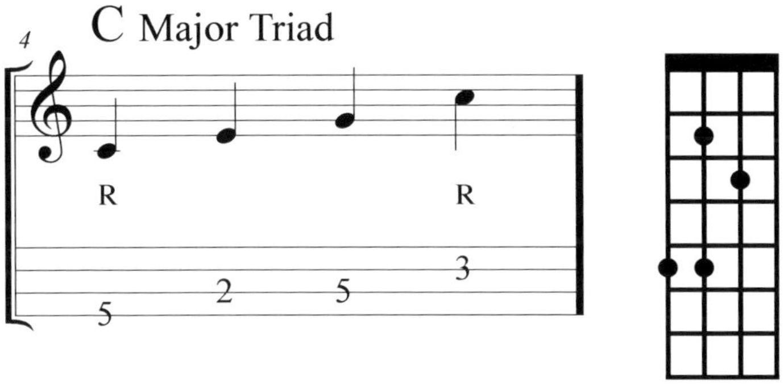

Scale Boxes Continued

Scale boxes can be moved anywhere around the fretboard and begun on any string. Here is an example of the two boxes on different strings and in different keys:

F Major Triad

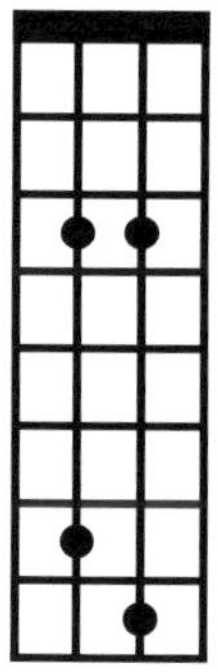

A♭ Major Triad

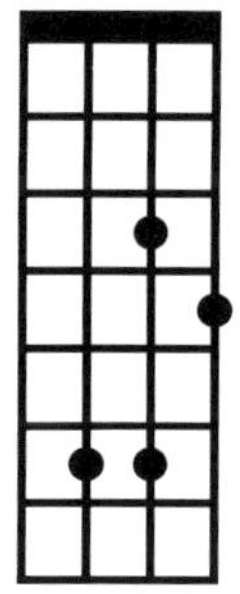

We can also cover all the strings by combining boxes. Notice how the two boxes share a note between them:

A Major Triad

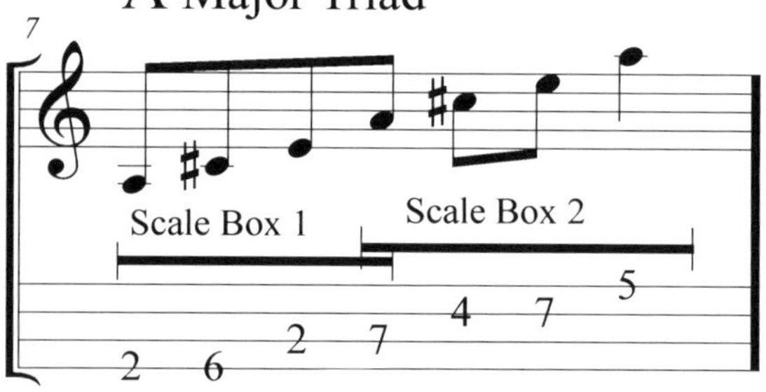

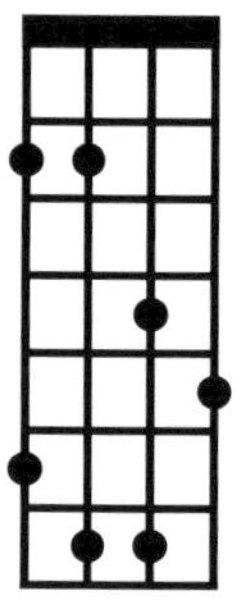

B Major Triad

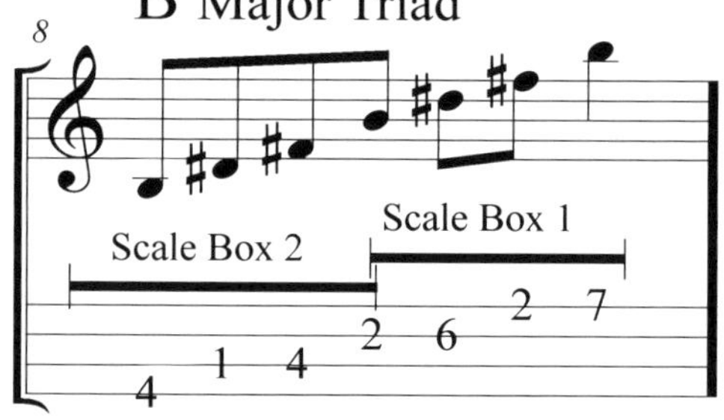

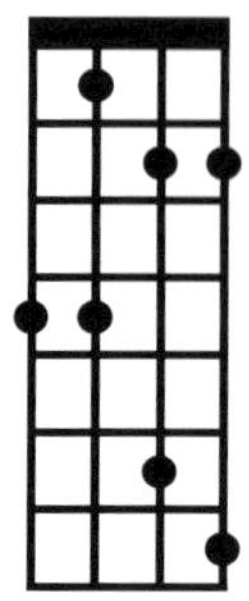

The next few chapters will focus on learning the location of each note on the fretboard, and the different ways to fill the scale boxes. Remember, once you learn one pattern, you can play it anywhere on the entire mandolin fretboard!

Visual Fretboard

The chart to the right displays all the notes on the mandolin. The four notes at the very top (in white circles) represent the open strings, and the numbers to the right represent frets.

Just like the fretboard charts that are displayed throughout this book, this chart is read as if you are holding the mandolin vertically and staring straight at the fretboard.

The chart is written with all flat notes, but keep in mind the enharmonic notes that are not written:

A♭ = G♯ | **B♭ = A♯** | **D♭ = C♯** |

E♭ = D♯ | **G♭ = F♯** |

Focus on memorizing this chart by first learning frets 1 – 5, then adding 6 – 9, then 10 – 12, 12 – 15, and 16 – 17 respectively. Use the fret markers (inlays) on your mandolin to help you.

It is very important to learn the notes on the mandolin when learning to improvise in closed position using scale boxes. In time, you will be able to visualize each scale box based on their starting note and position on the fretboard.

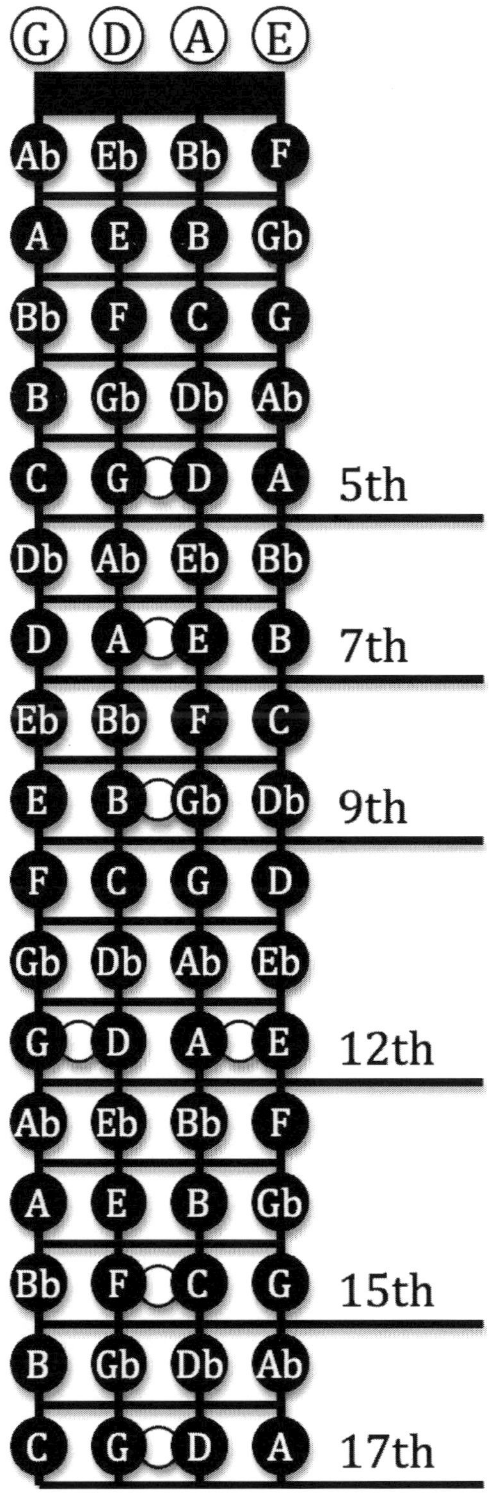

Scale Box Patterns

The next few pages will show the different chords and scales with which you can fill your scale boxes, followed by 4 patterns. Each scale box is marked with a bracket and number (for Scale Box 1 or 2). Each set of patterns is accompanied by a practice progression to help you learn.

Major Triad Patterns

Scale Box 1

Scale Box 2

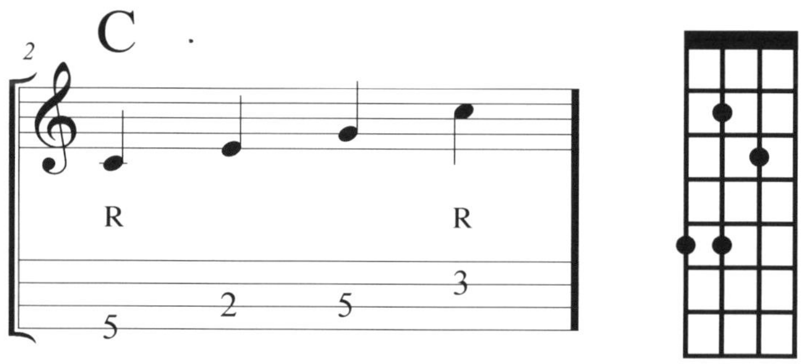

Pattern 1

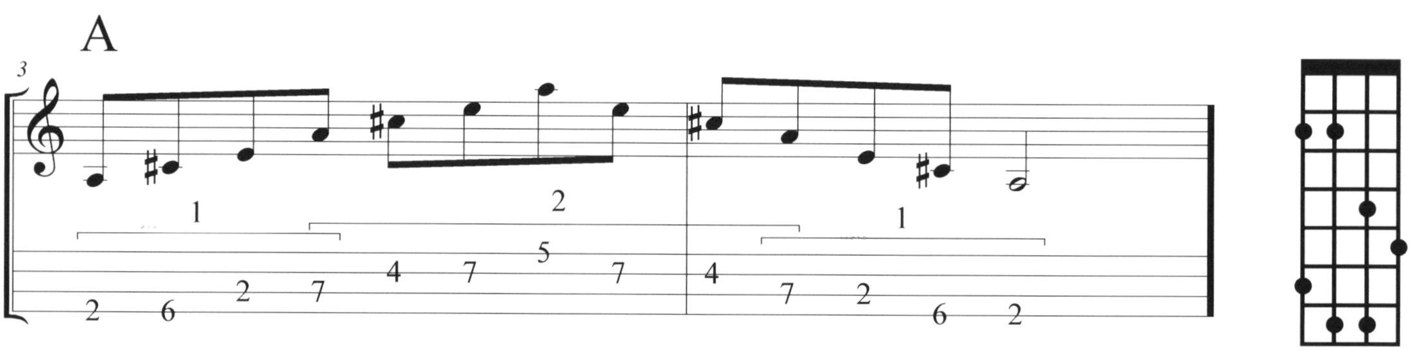

Pattern 2

Major Triad Patterns Continued

The notes outside the scale patterns are what I call **fragments**. If the mandolin had more strings, the fragments would form full scale boxes. As you learn each pattern, the fragments around the scale boxes will become easier to memorize.

Pattern 3

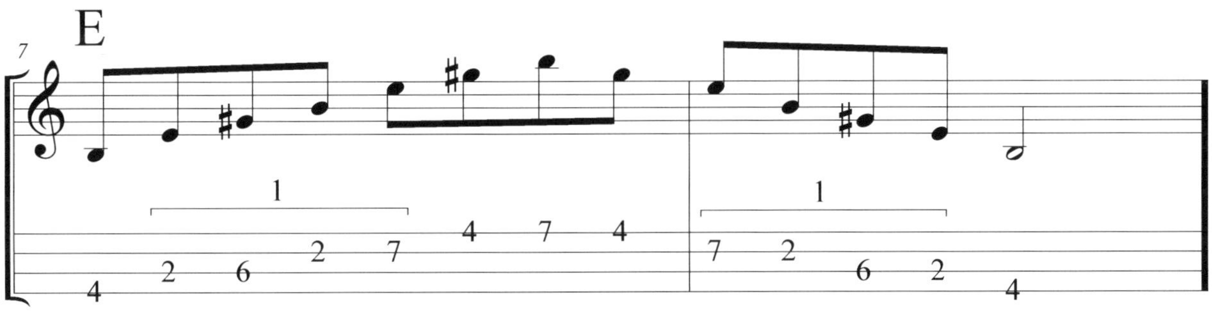

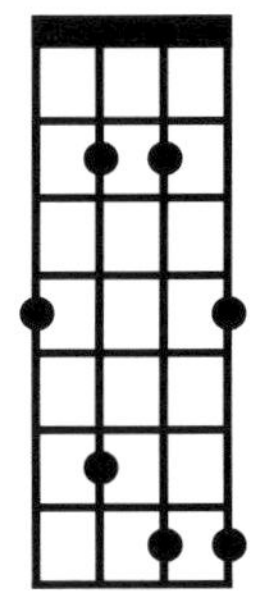

Pattern 4

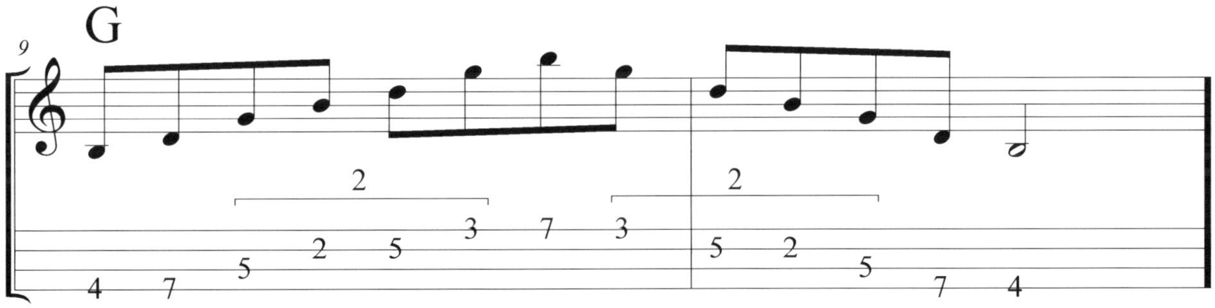

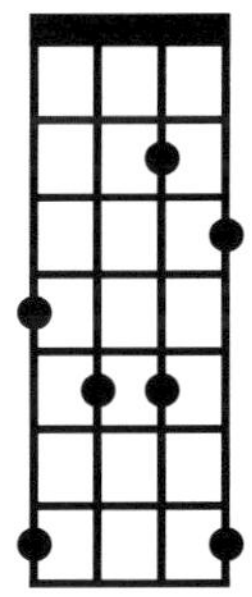

15

Here is a practice progression using triad patterns. Just like before, learn this solo and then practice writing your own:

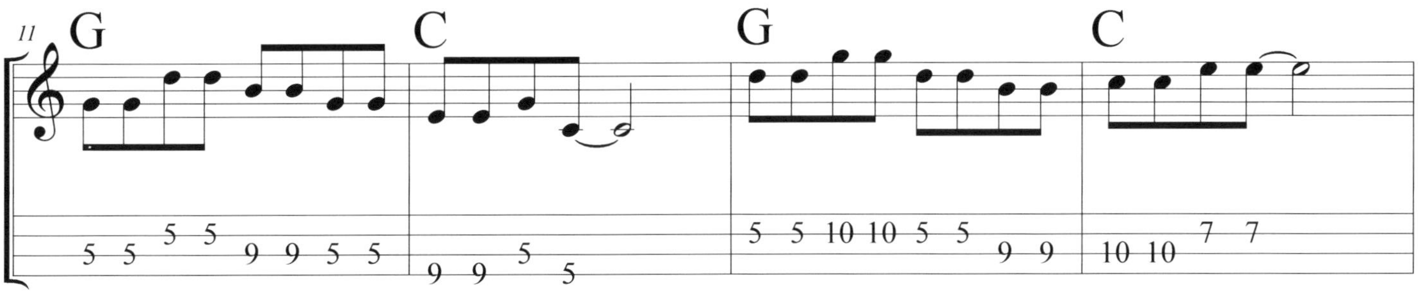

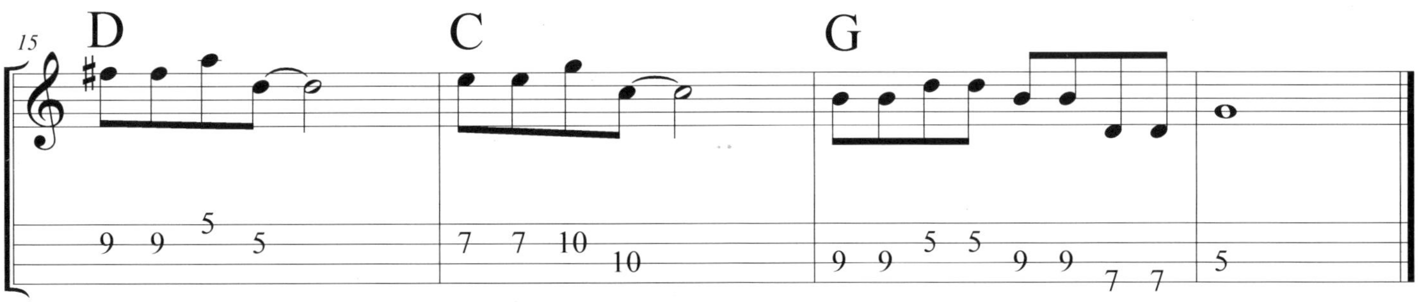

Minor Triad Patterns

Below are the minor triad scale boxes. Notice that the only difference between the major and minor triad is the second note (the "3rd") just moves down a fret. Learn the examples below and keep in mind the similarities between major and minor triads.

Scale Box 1

A Minor

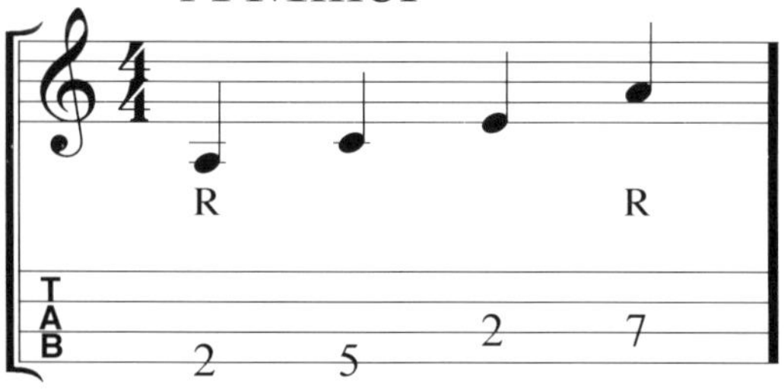

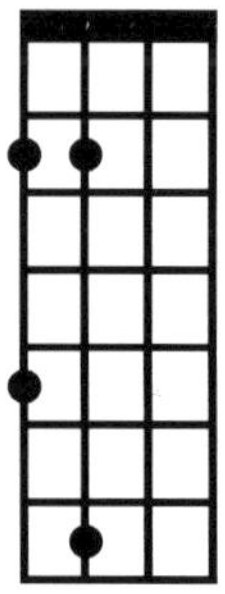

Scale Box 2

C Minor

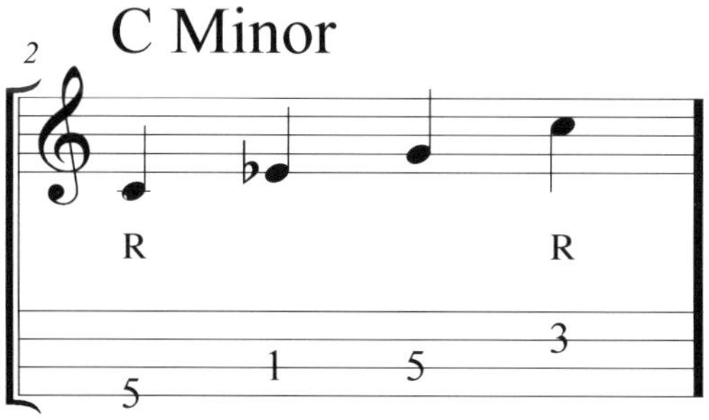

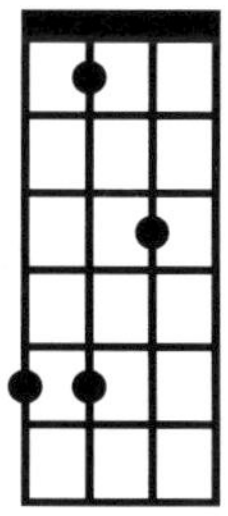

Pattern 1

A Minor

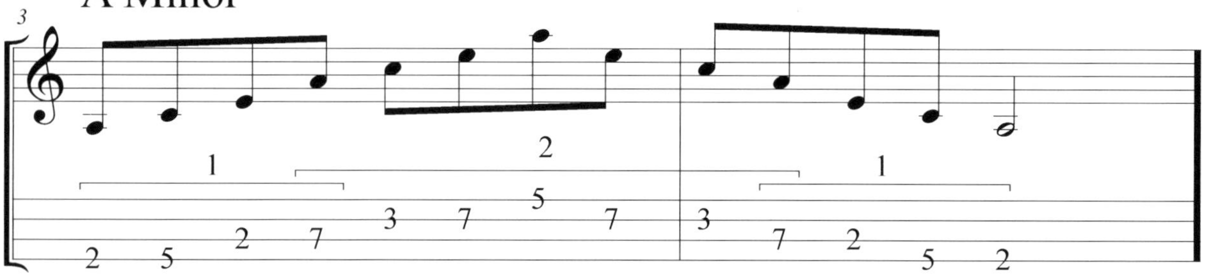

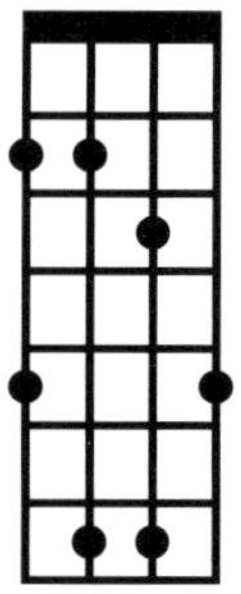

Pattern 2

C Minor

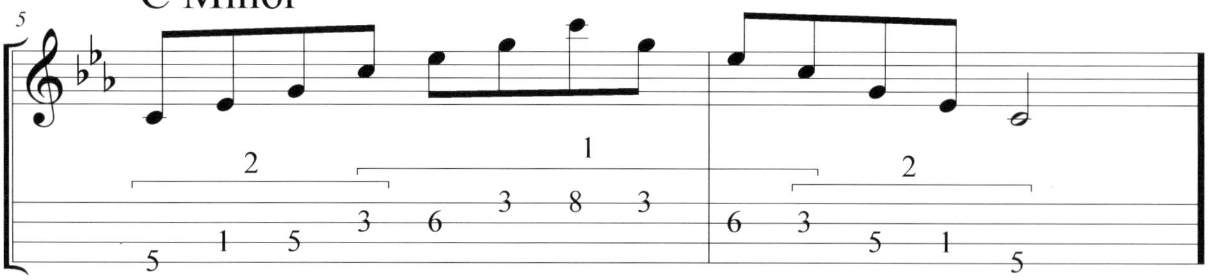

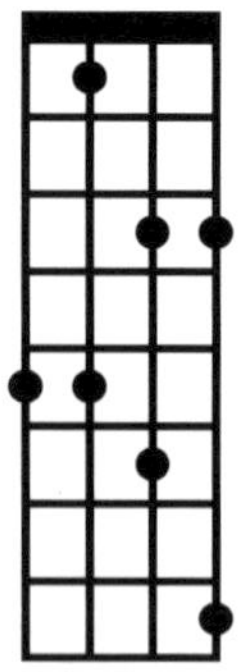

Minor Triad Patterns Continued

Pattern 3

E Minor

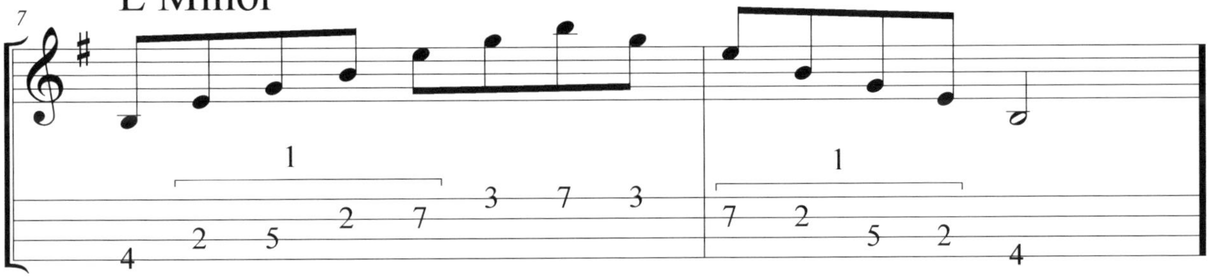

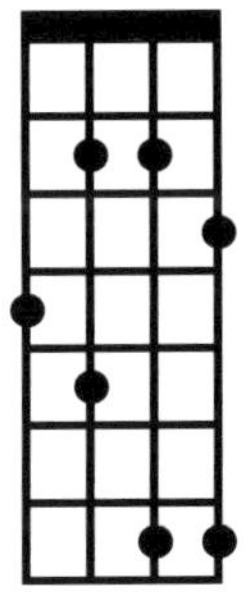

Pattern 4

G Minor

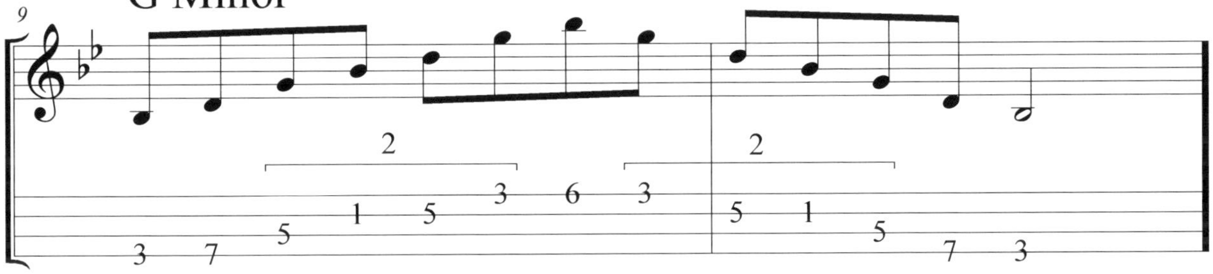

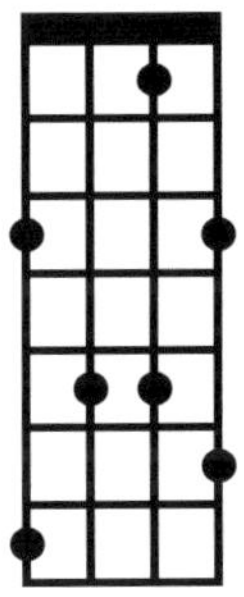

Practice Progression

16

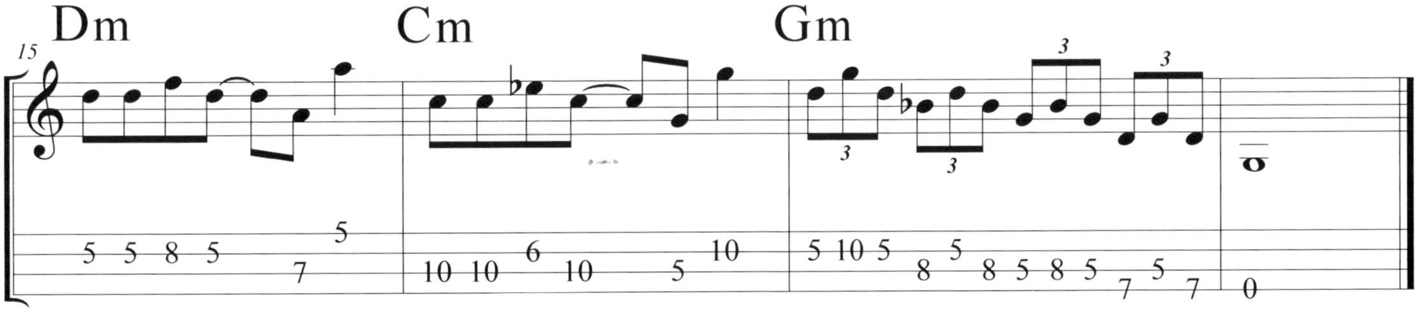

Major Pentatonic Scale Boxes

The major pentatonic scale boxes take the major triad chord tones and add two more notes to create a pentatonic scale.

Scale Box 1

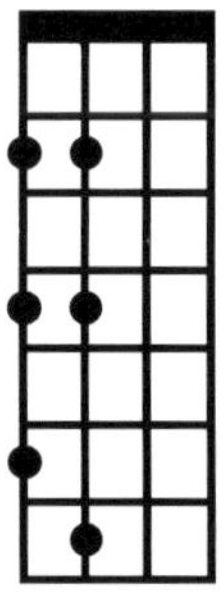

Scale Box 2

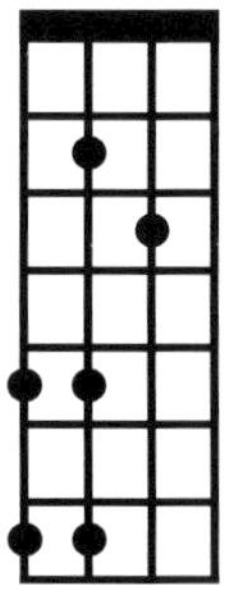

Pattern 1

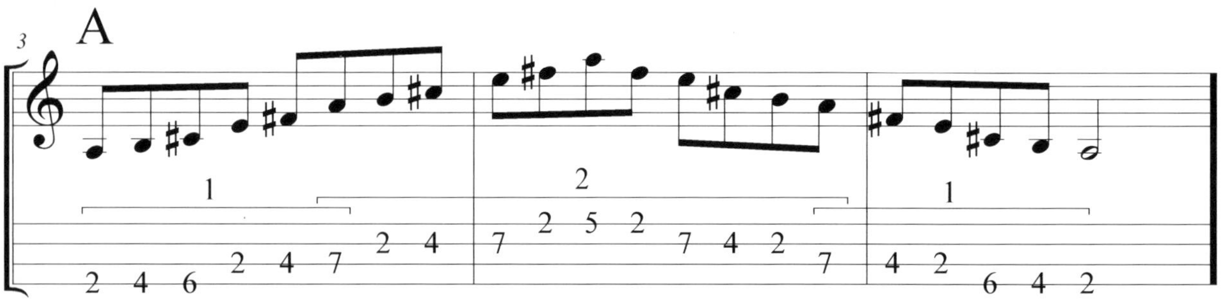

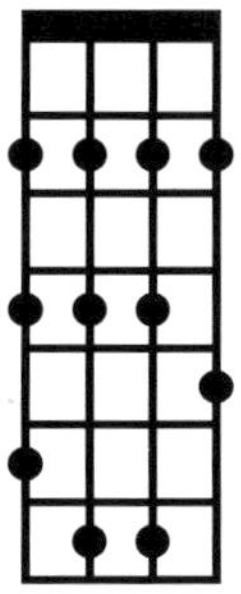

Pattern 2

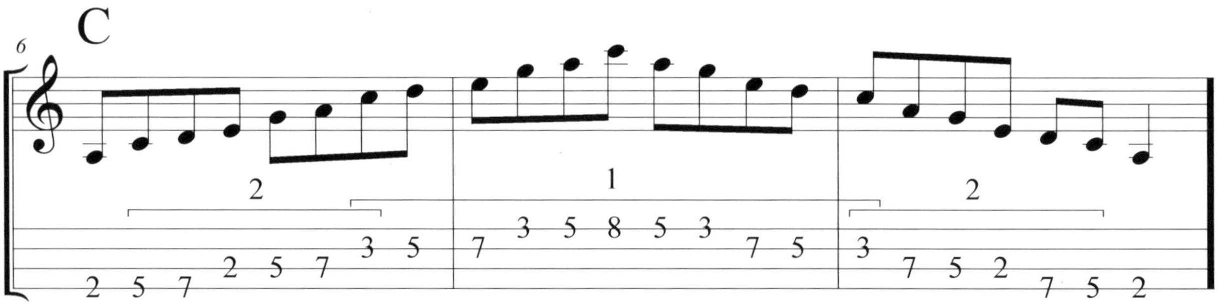

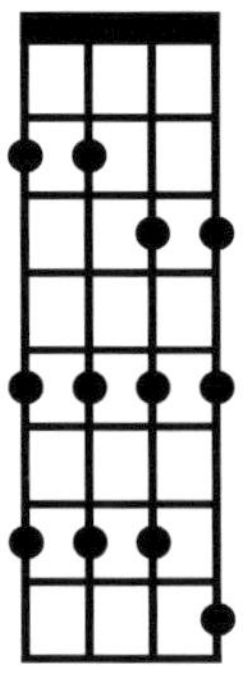

Major Pentatonic Patterns Continued

Pattern 3

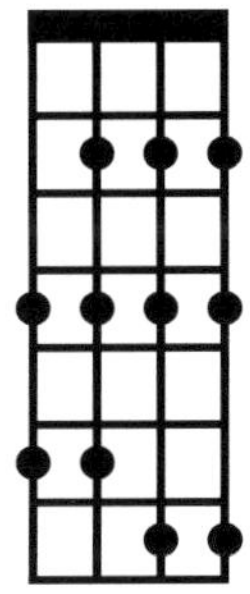

Pattern 4

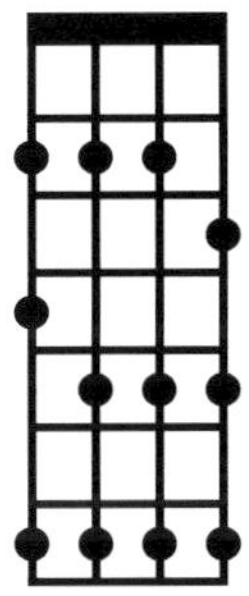

Practice Progression

17

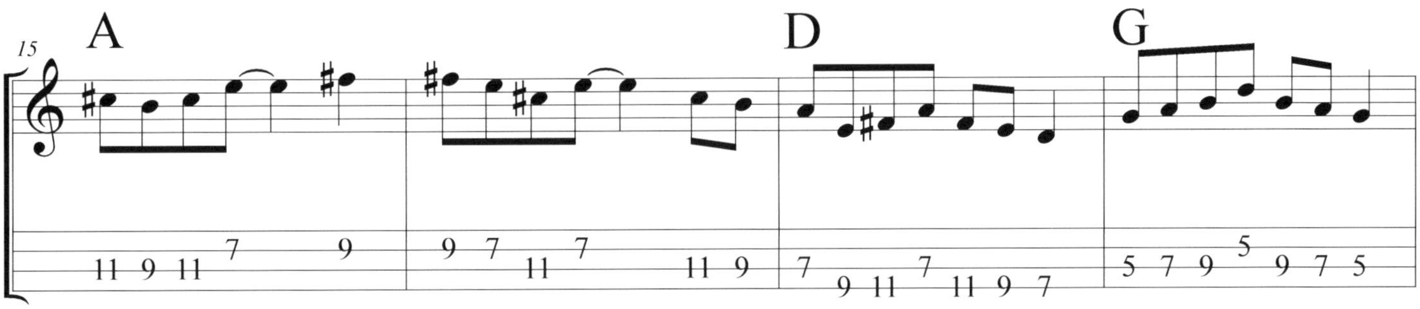

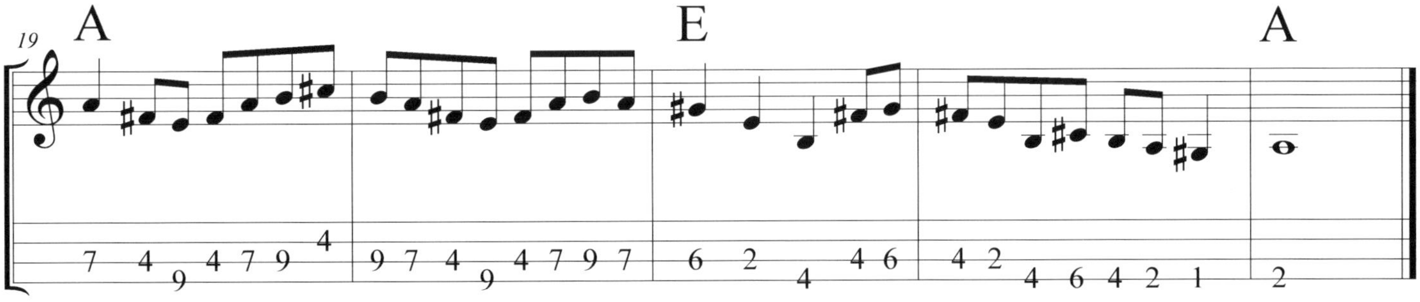

Minor Pentatonic Patterns

Now let's add notes to the minor triad to make the minor pentatonic patterns:

Scale Box 1

A Minor

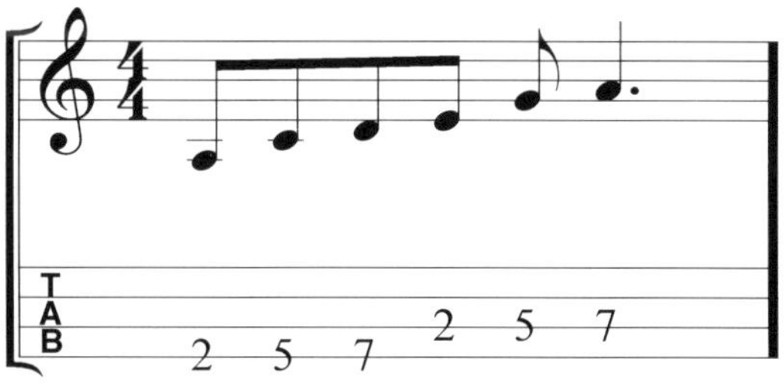

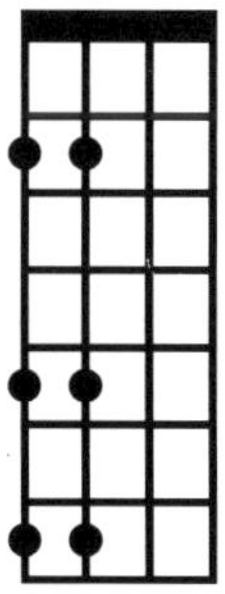

Scale Box 2

C Minor

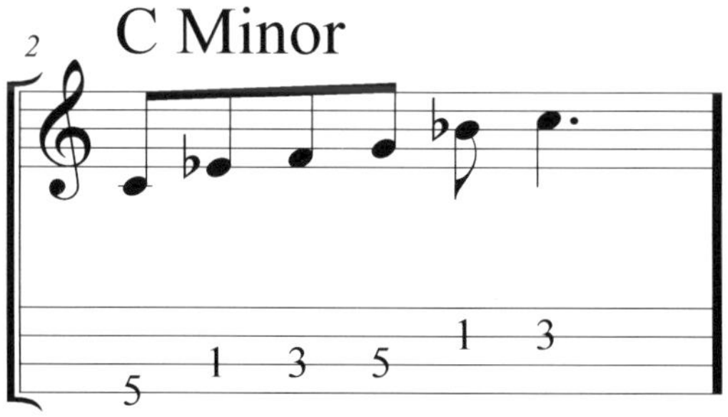

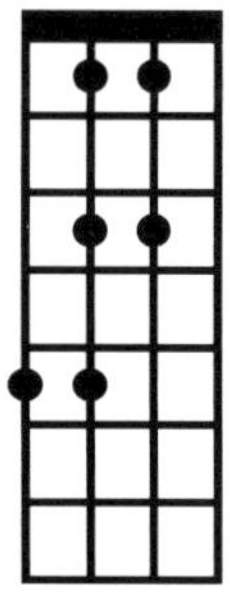

Pattern 1

A Minor

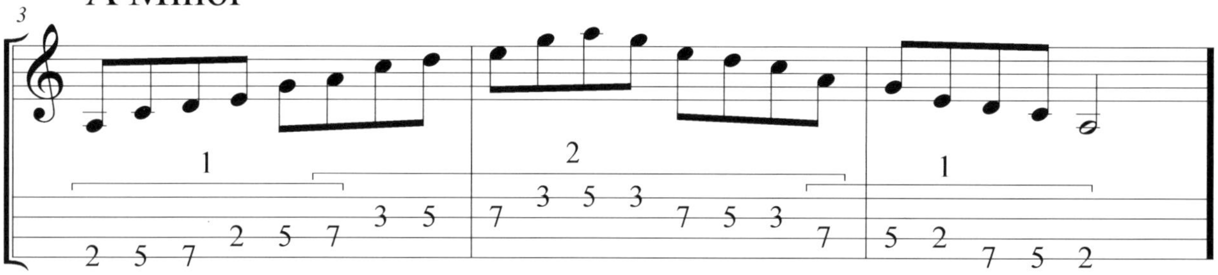

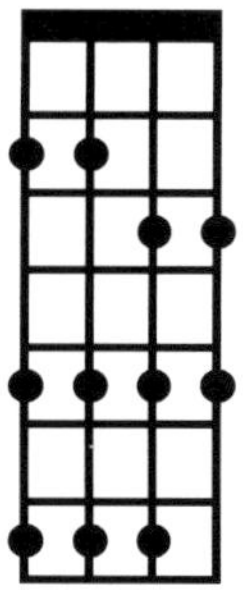

Pattern 2

C Minor

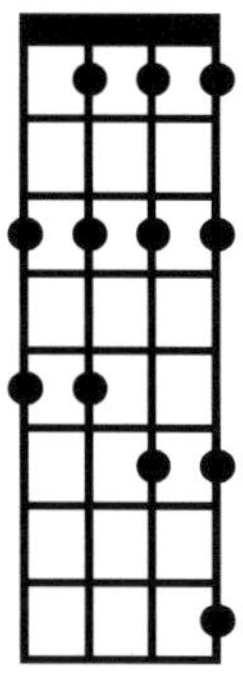

Minor Pentatonic Patterns Continued

Pattern 3

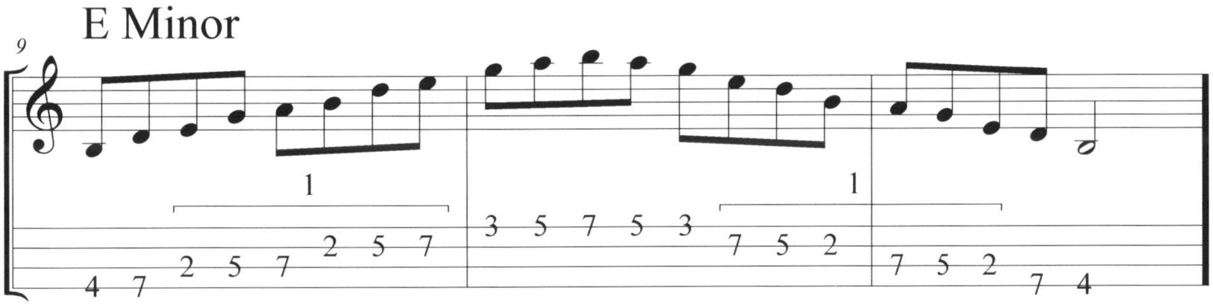

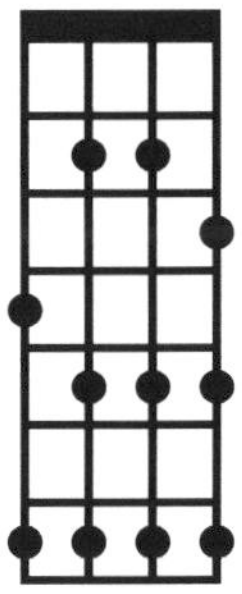

Pattern 4

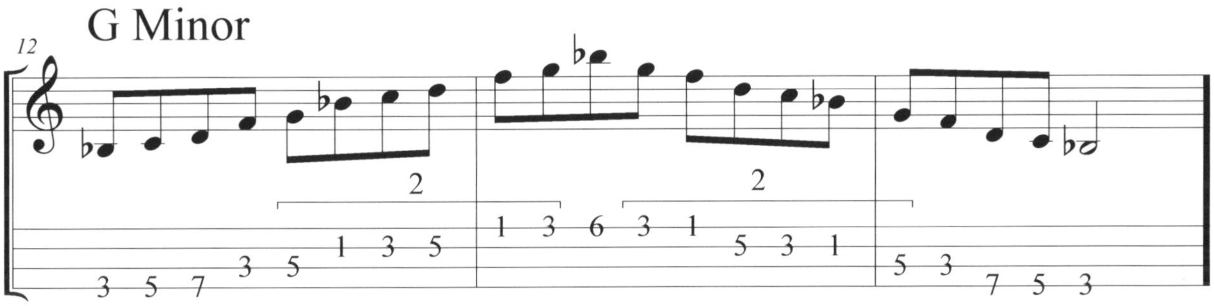

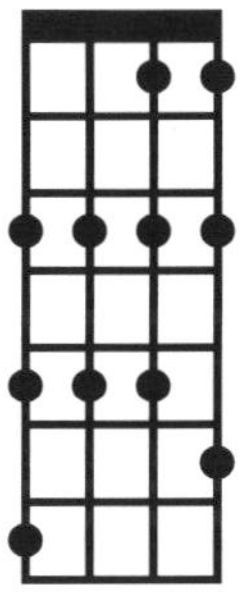

Practice Progression

18

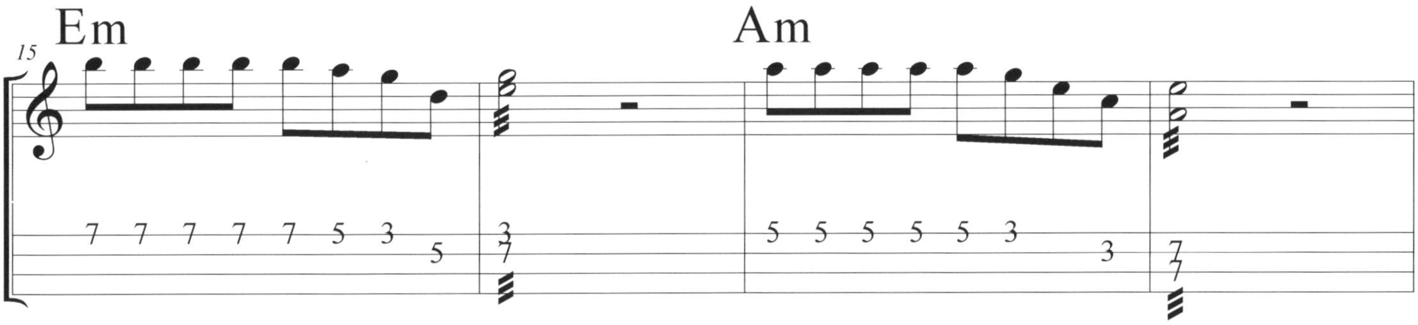

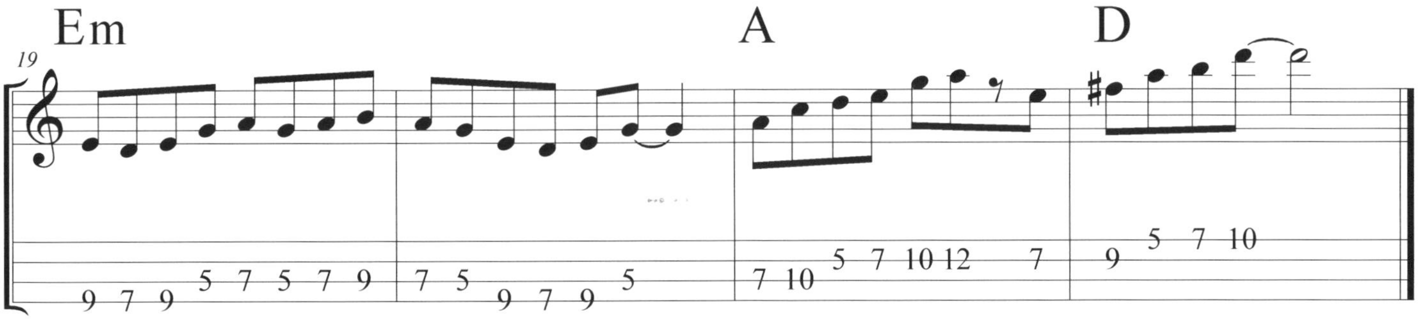

Passing Tones Between the 2nd and 3rd Notes

Here are the different patterns of major pentatonic scales with passing tones between the 2nd and 3rd notes:

Scale Box 1

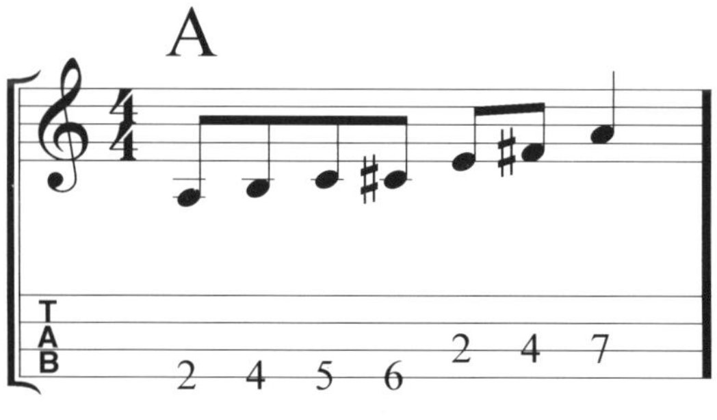

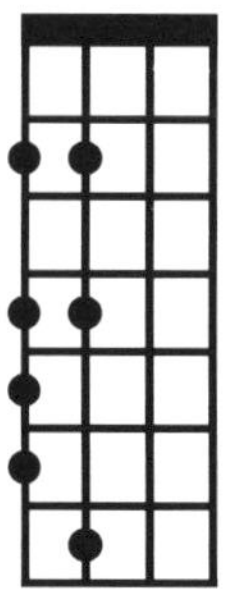

Scale Box 2

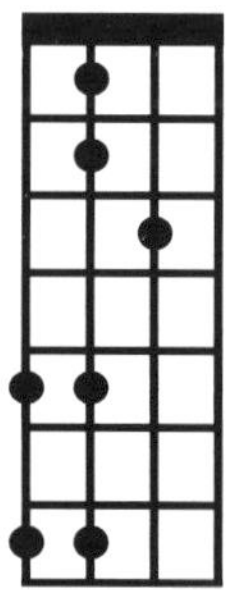

Pattern 1

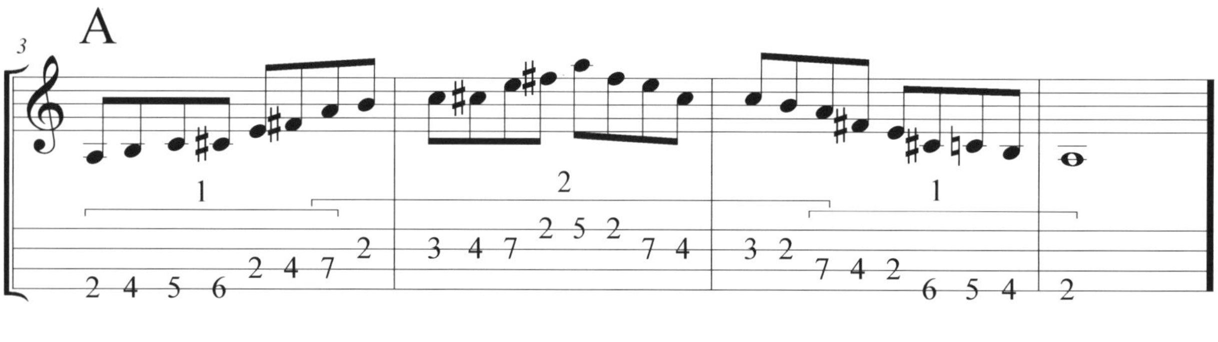

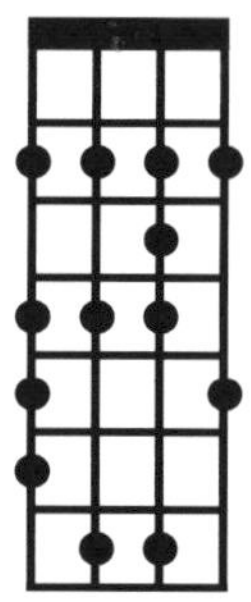

Pattern 2

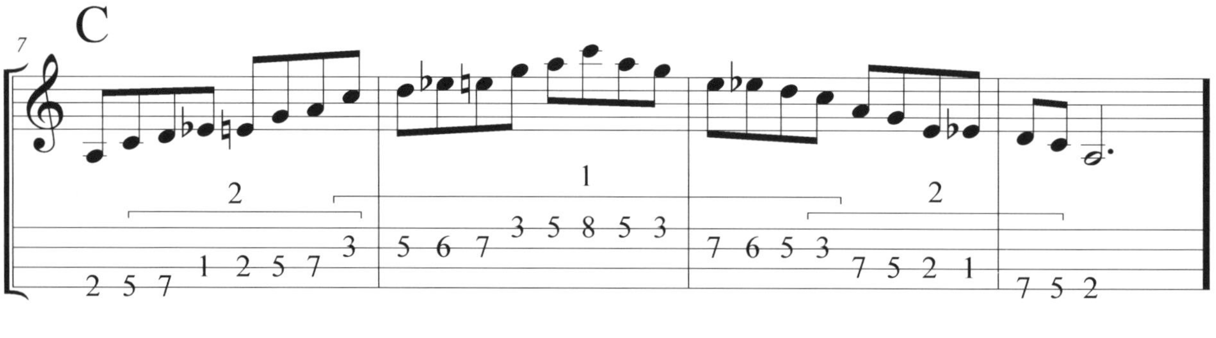

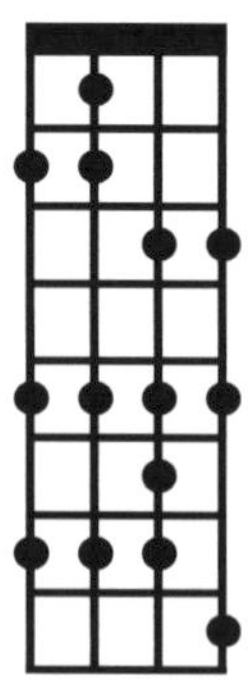

Passing Tones Between the 2nd and 3rd Notes Continued

Pattern 3

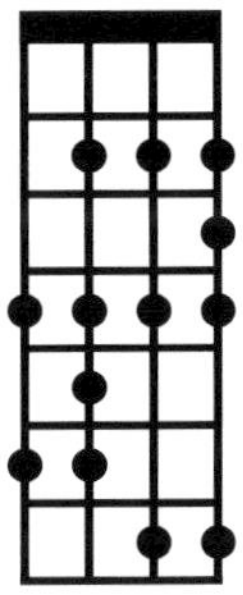

Pattern 4

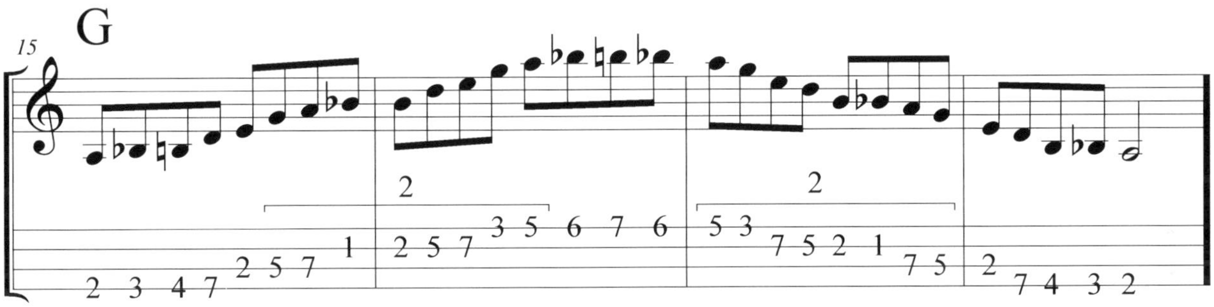

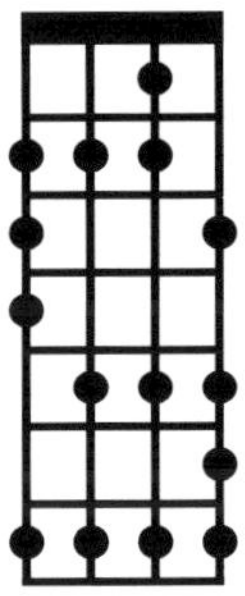

Practice Progression

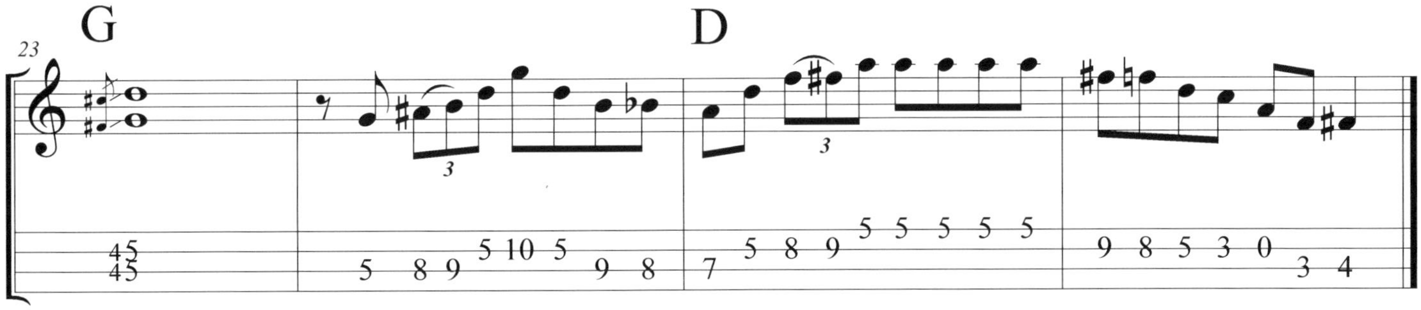

Passing Tones Between the 3rd and 5th Notes

Here are the different patterns of major pentatonic scales with passing tones between the 3rd and 5th notes:

Scale Box 1

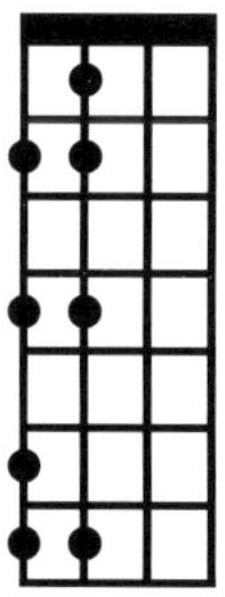

Scale Box 2

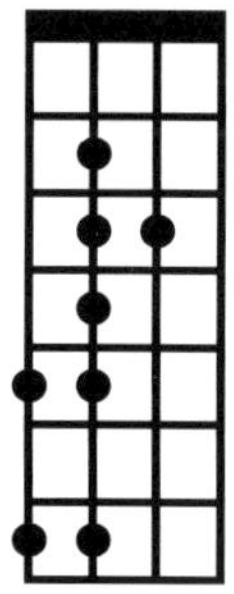

Pattern 1

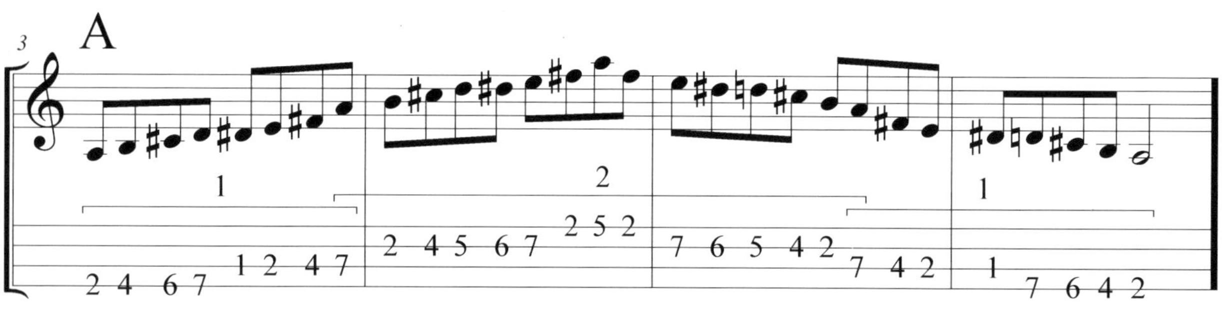

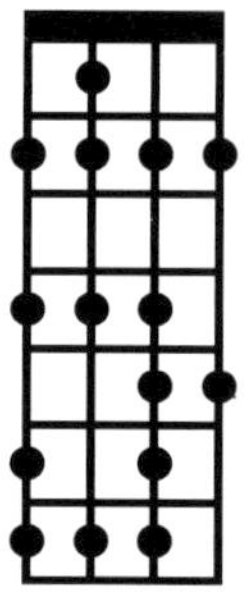

Pattern 2

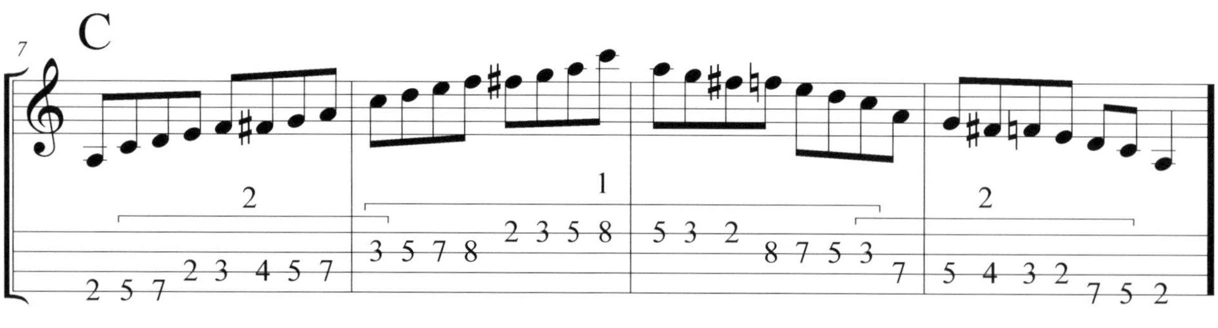

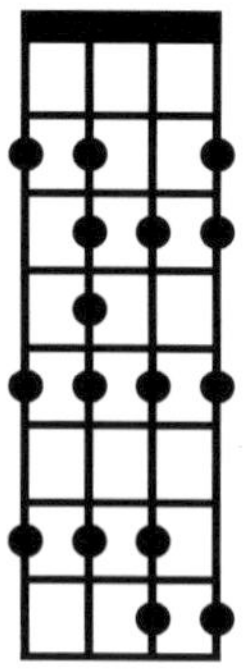

Passing Tones Between the 3rd and 5th Notes Continued

Pattern 3

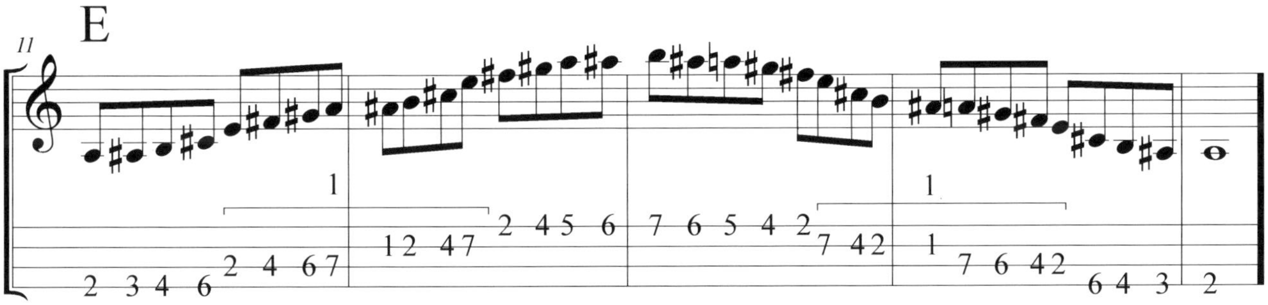

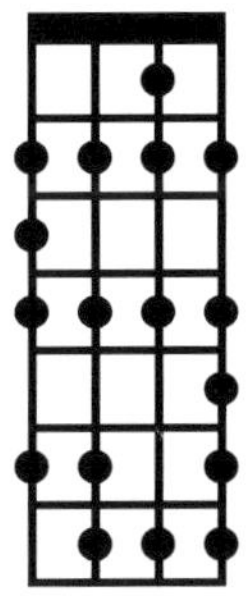

Pattern 4

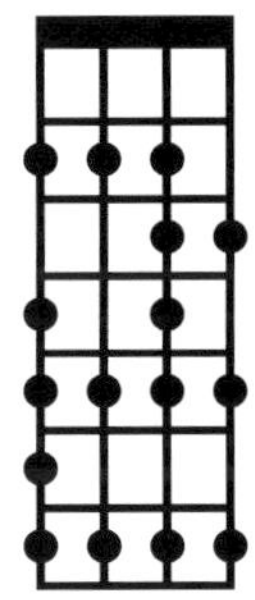

Practice Progression

20

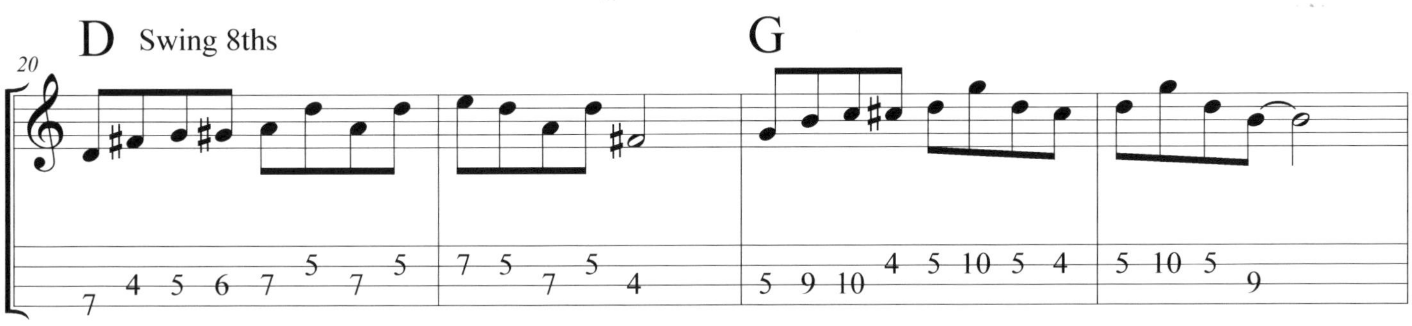

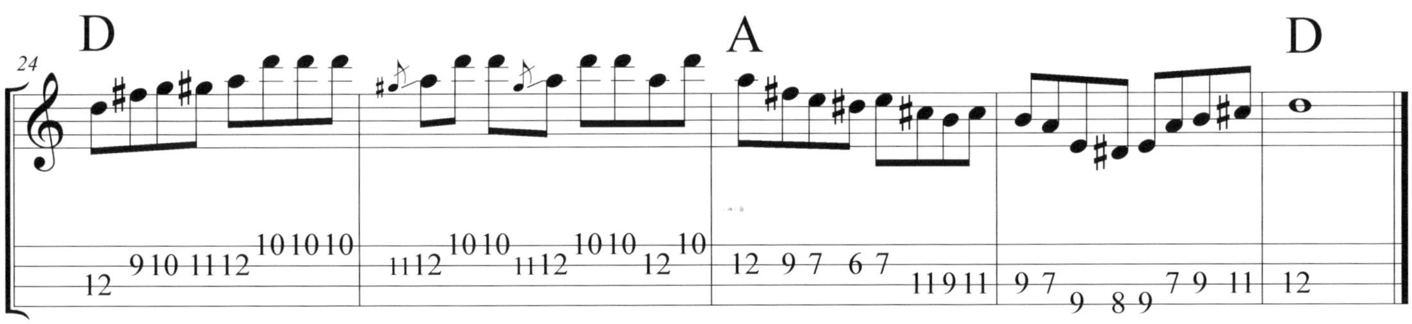

The Minor Pentatonic Blues Scale

Here is the minor pentatonic scale with added notes to form the blues scale:

Scale Box 1

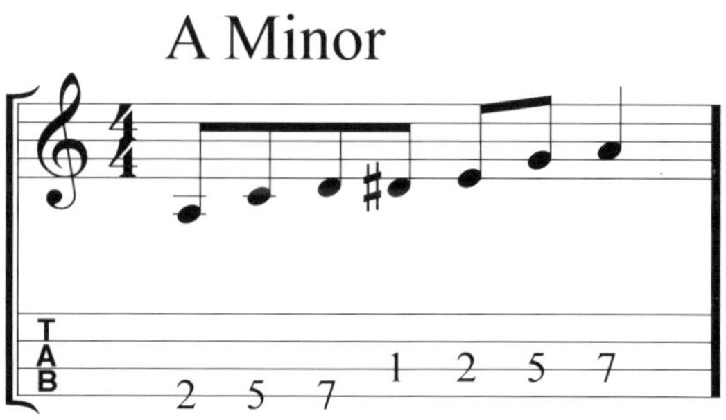

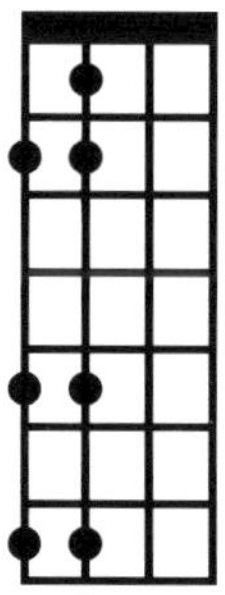

Scale Box 2

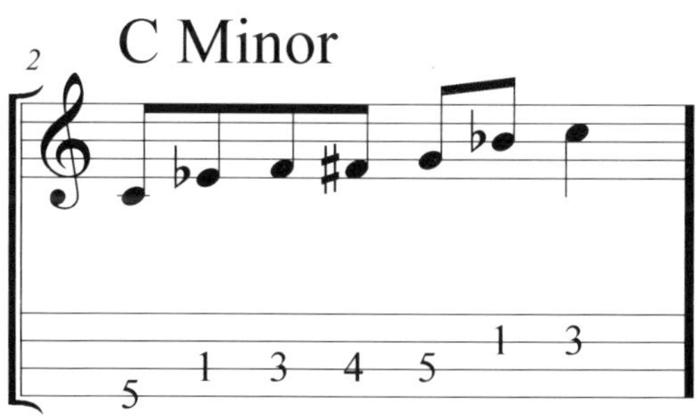

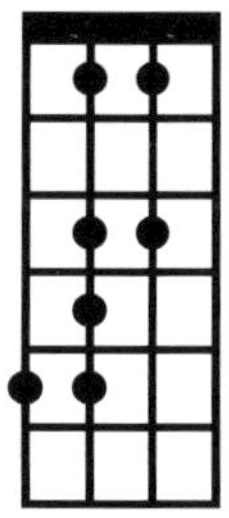

Pattern 1

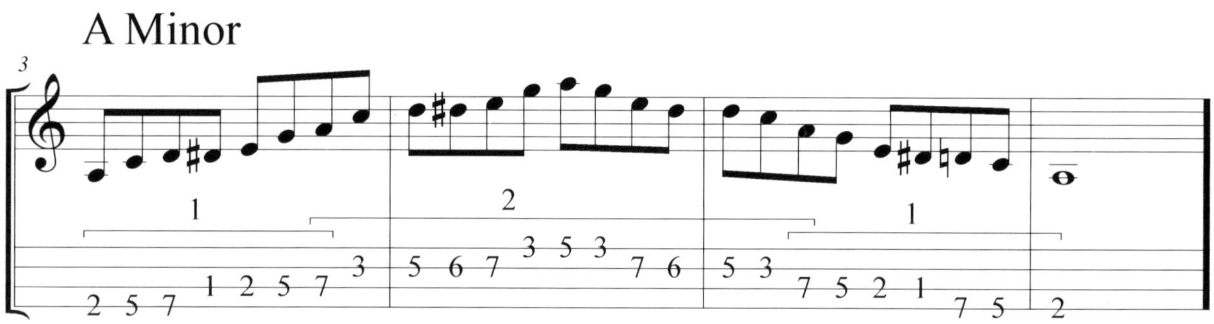

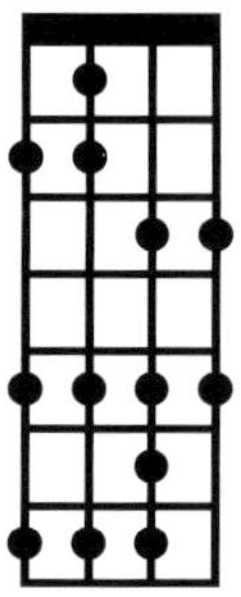

Pattern 2

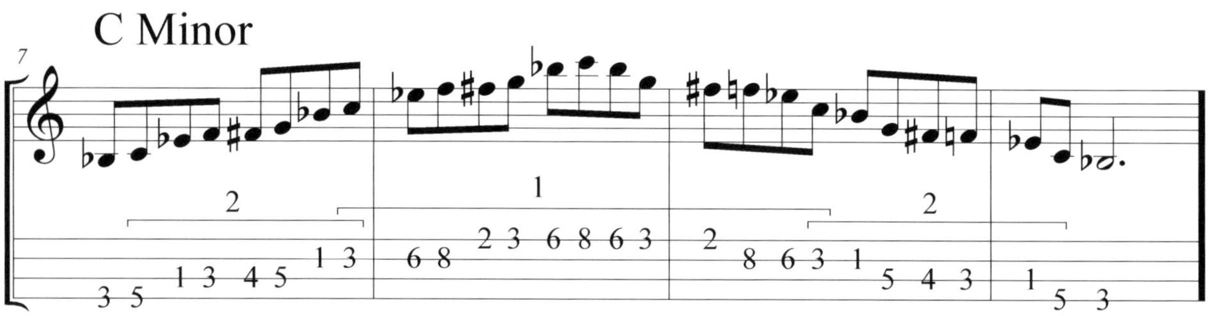

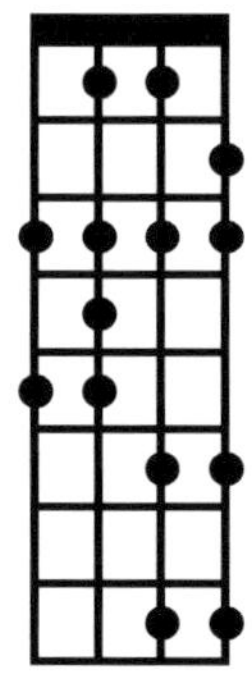

Minor Pentatonic Blues Scale Continued

Pattern 3

E Minor

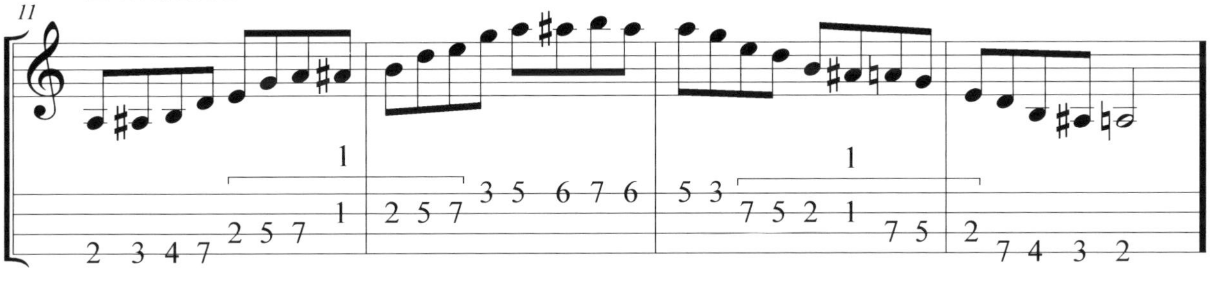

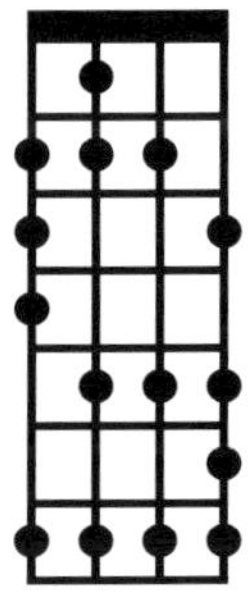

Pattern 4

G Minor

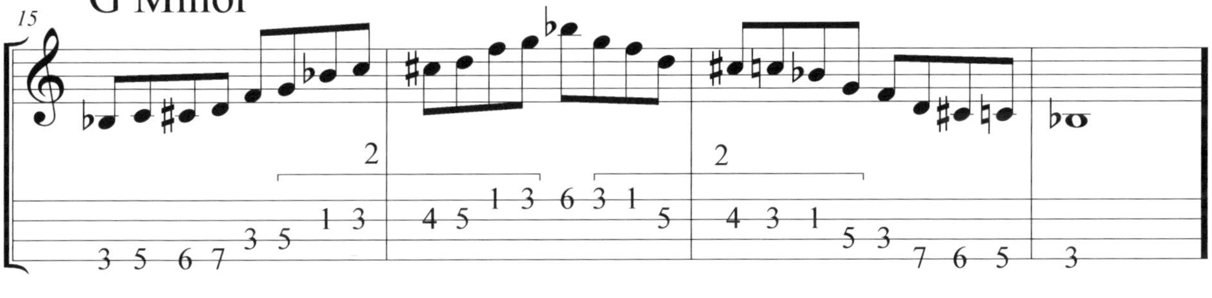

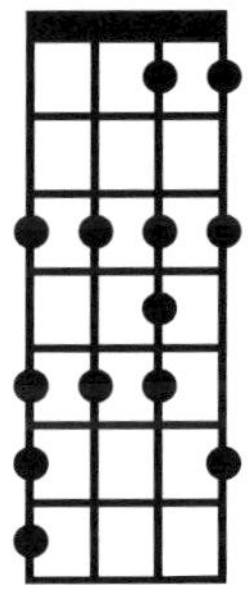

Practice Progression 21

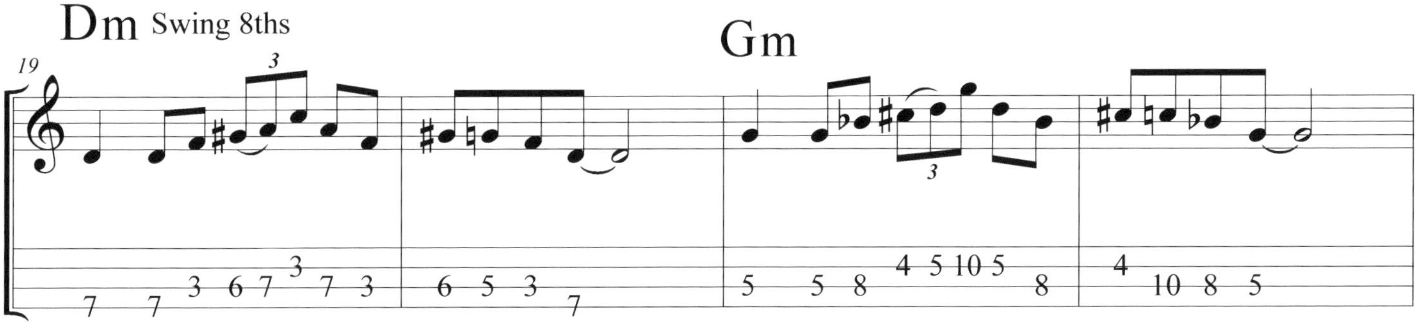

Dominant 7th Chord Tones

Next we will look at adding a note to the major triad to create the dominant 7th chord.

Scale Box 1

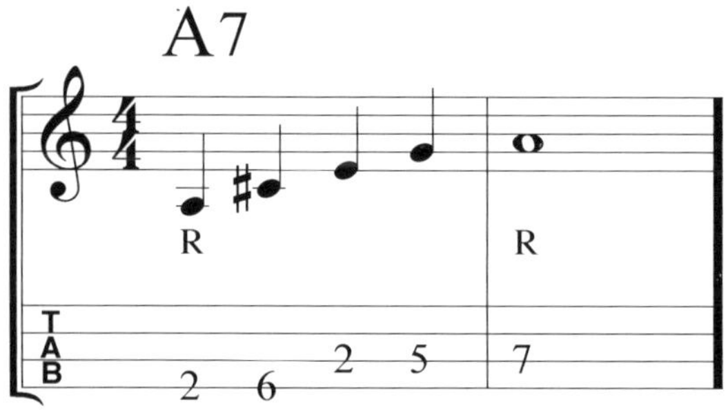

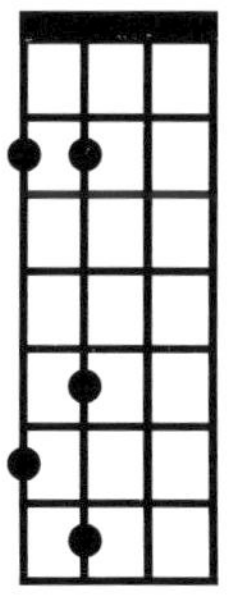

Scale Box 2

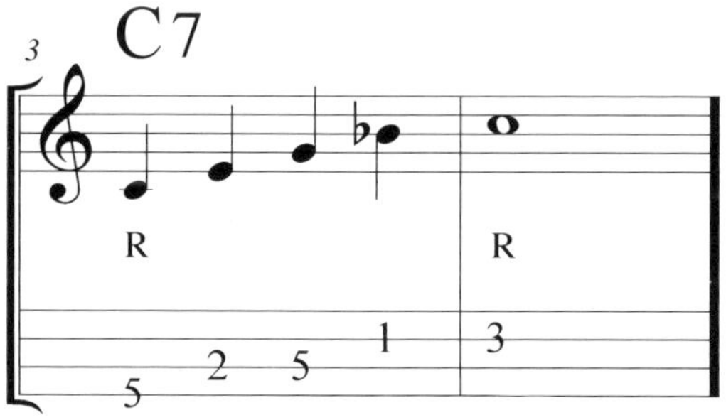

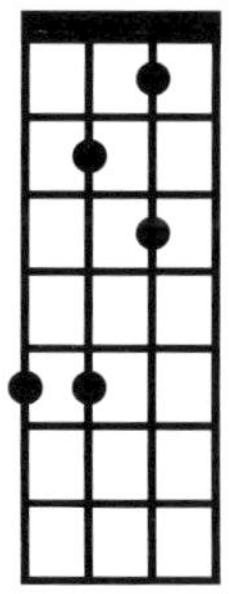

Pattern 1

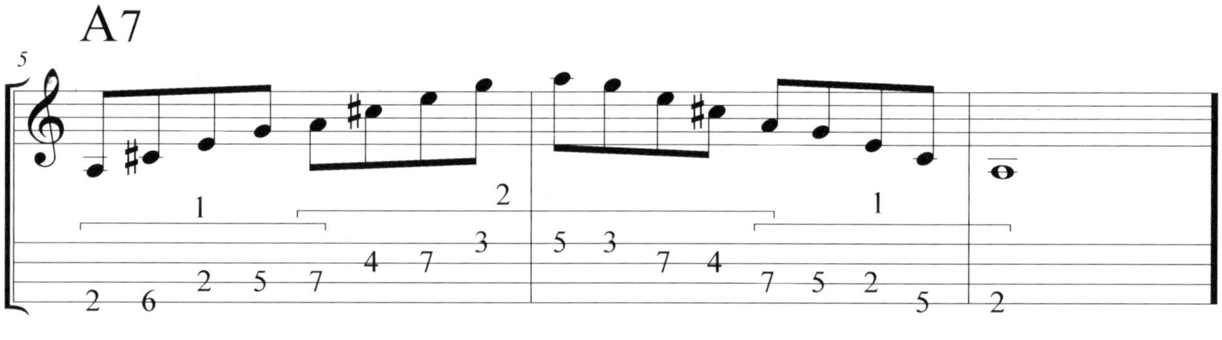

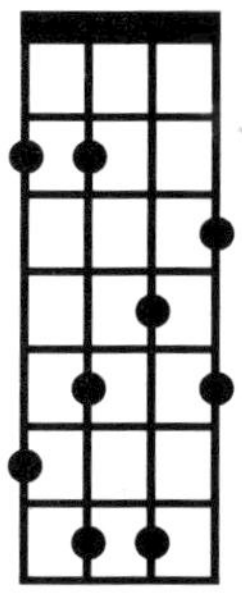

Pattern 2

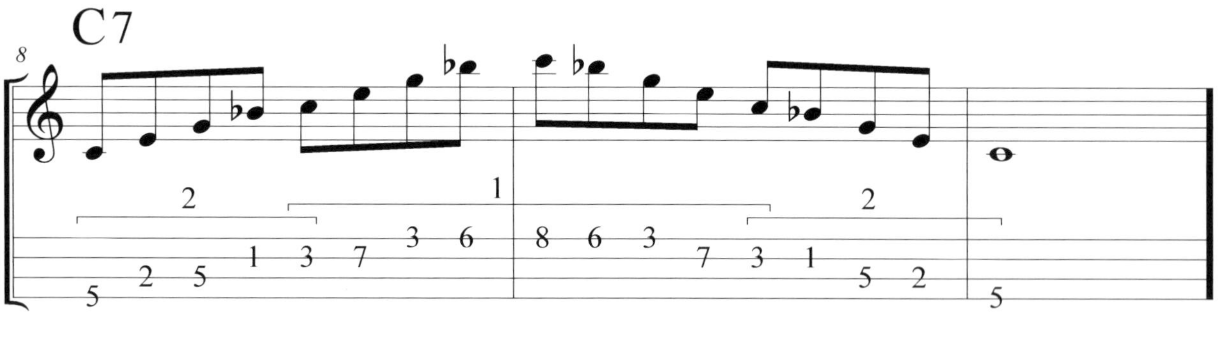

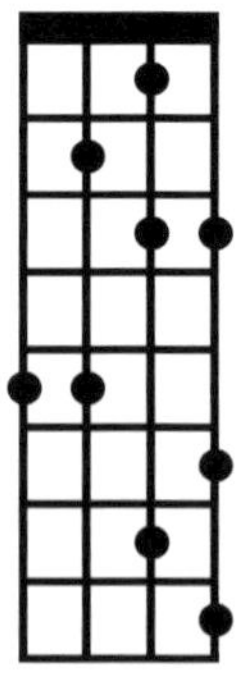

Pattern 3

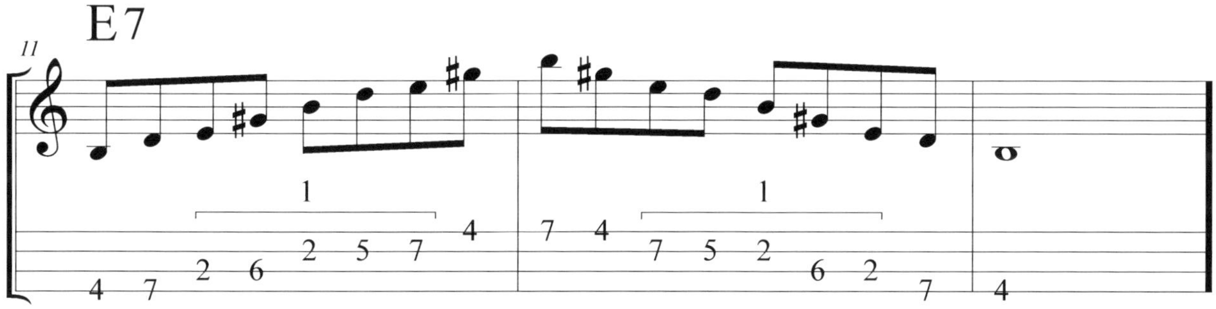

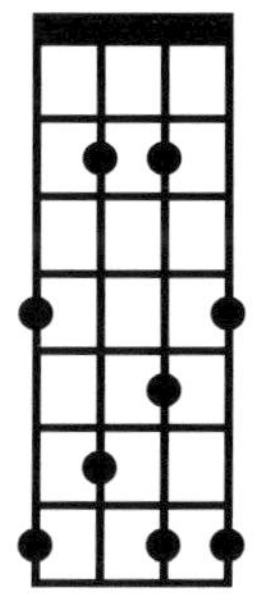

Pattern 4

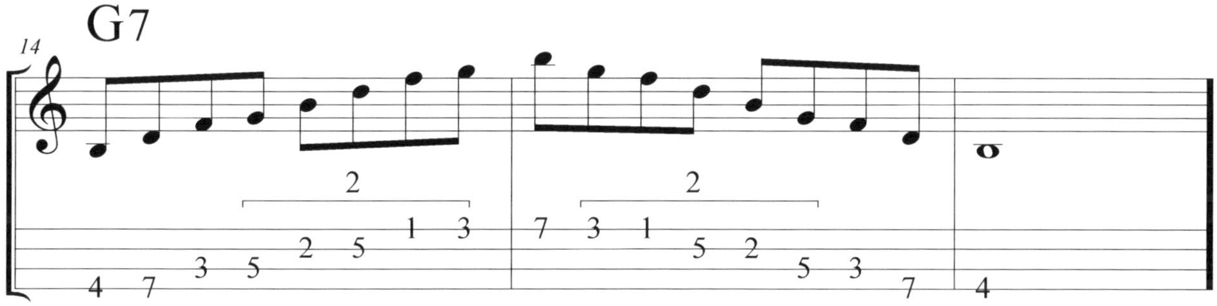

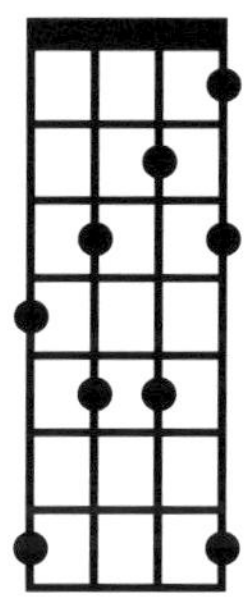

Practice Progression

22

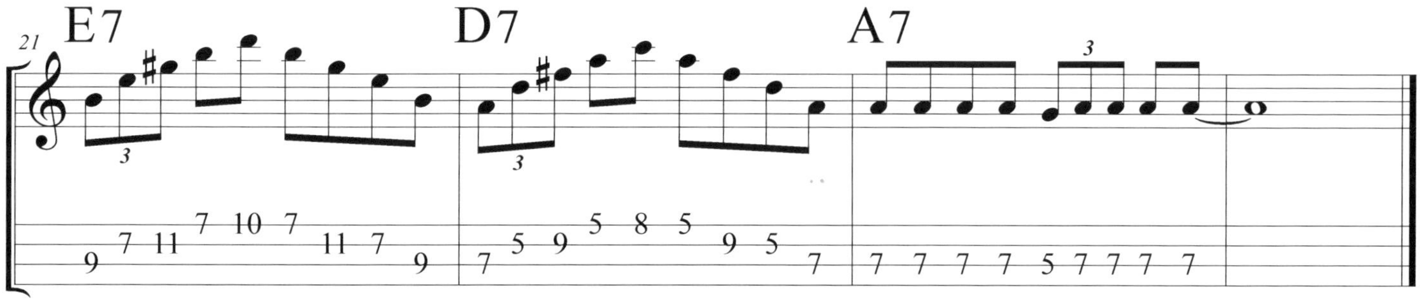

Major Scale

Here is the closed-position major scale:

Scale Box 1

Scale Box 2

Pattern 1

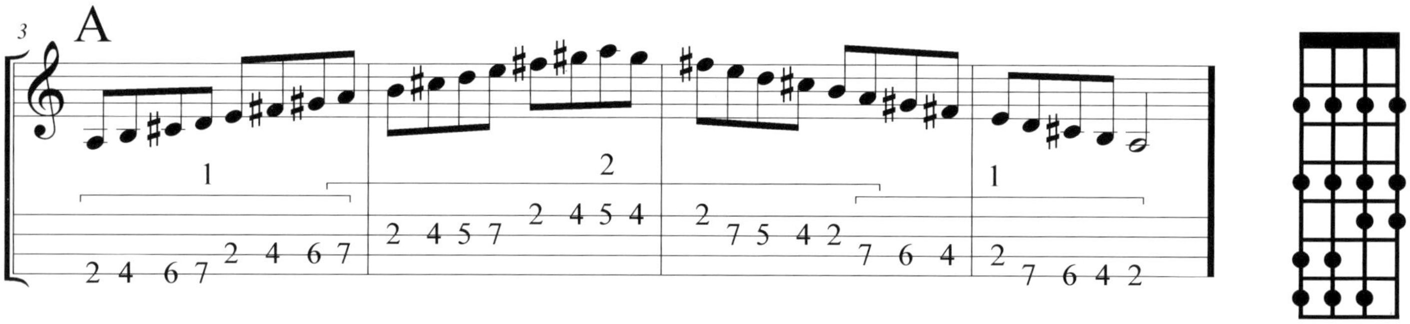

Pattern 2

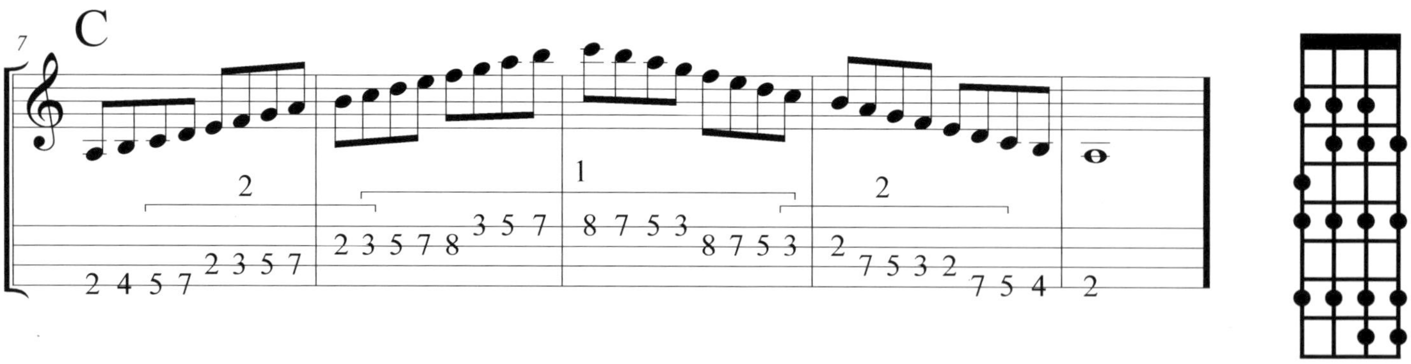

Major Scale Patterns Continued

Pattern 3

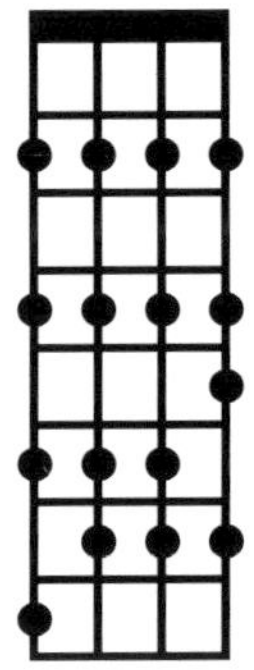

Pattern 4

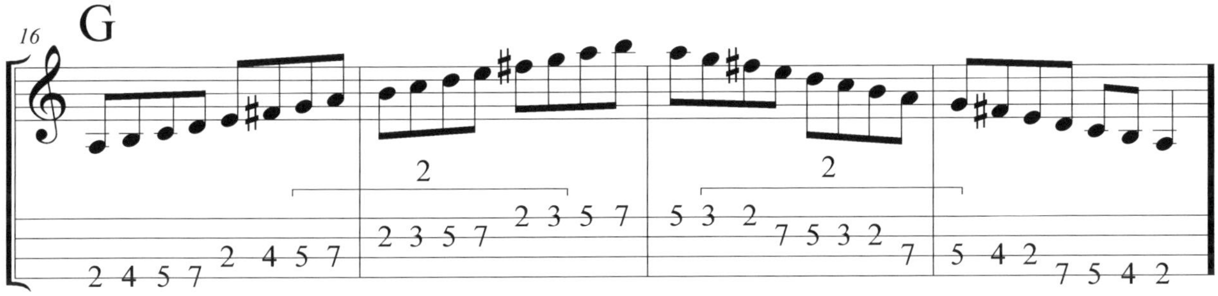

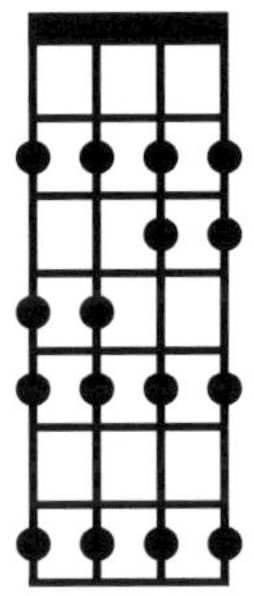

Practice Progression

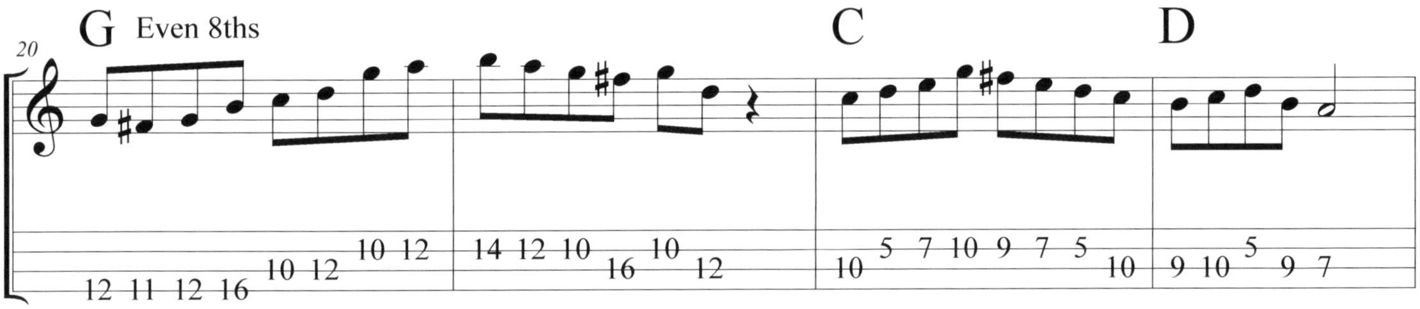

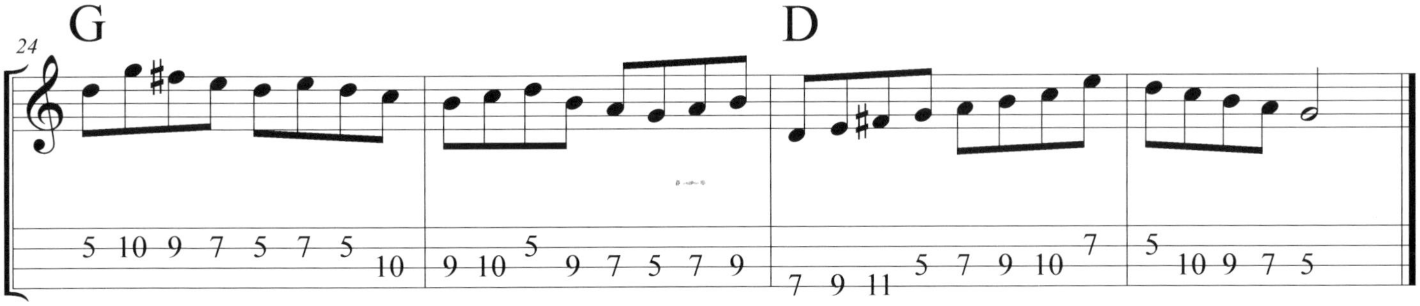

The Natural Minor Scales

The final scale boxes we'll examine in this chapter are for the natural minor scale.

Scale Box 1

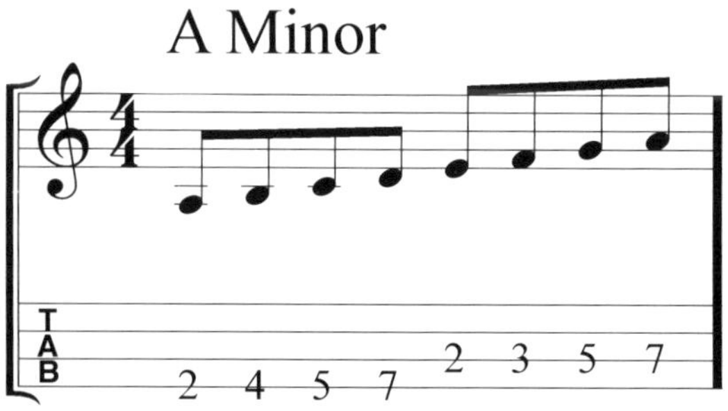

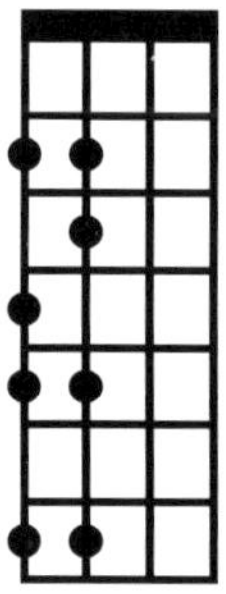

Scale Box 2

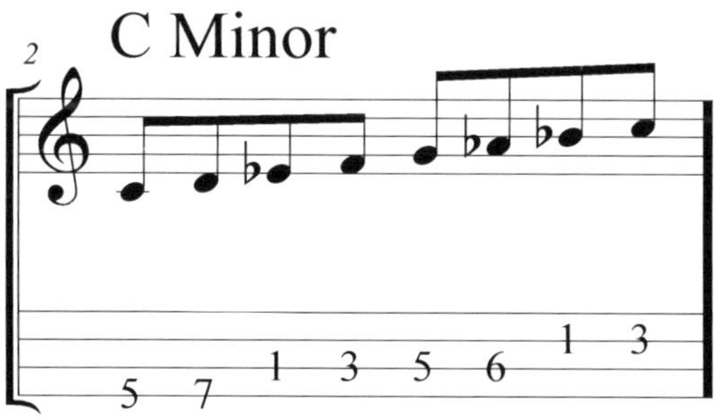

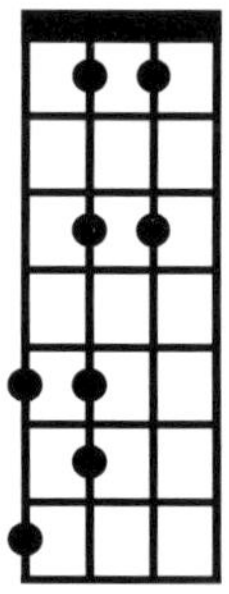

Pattern 1

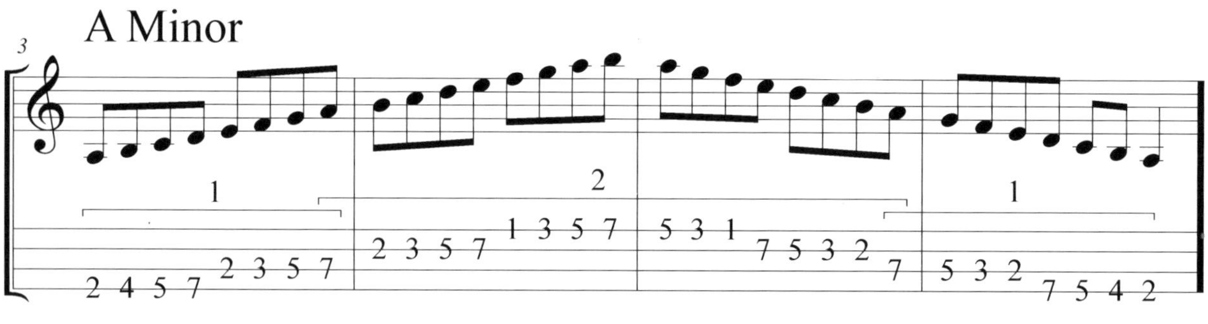

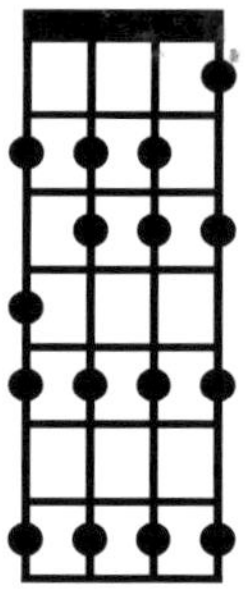

Pattern 2

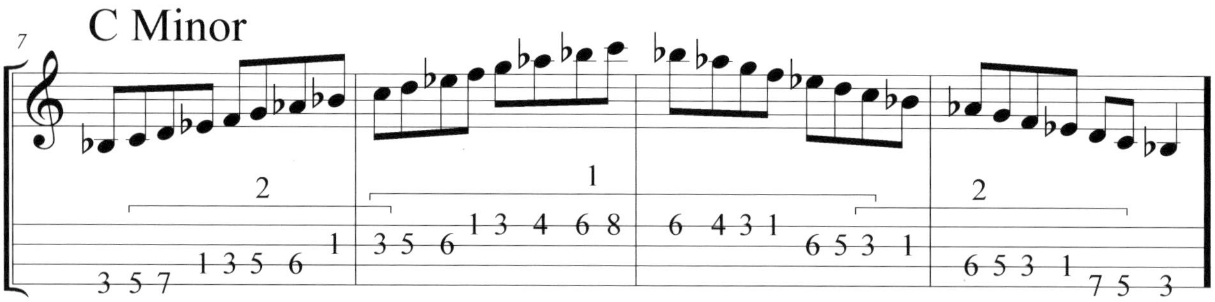

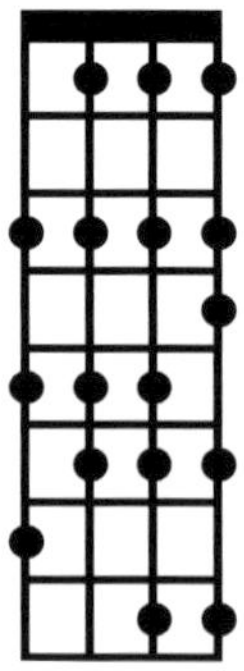

Natural Minor Scale Patterns Continued

Pattern 3

E Minor

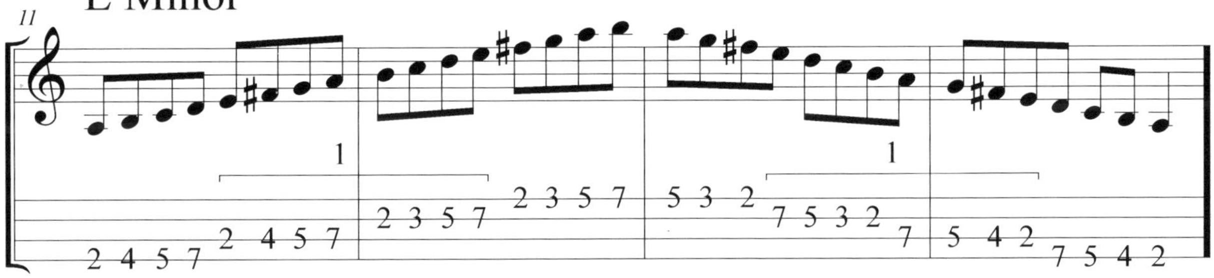

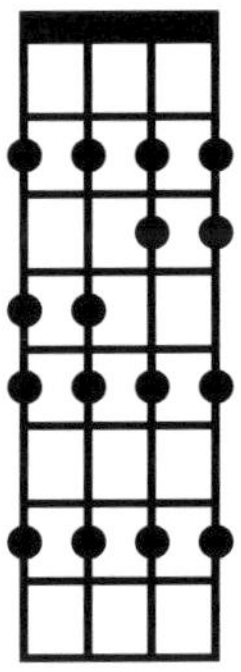

Pattern 4

G Minor

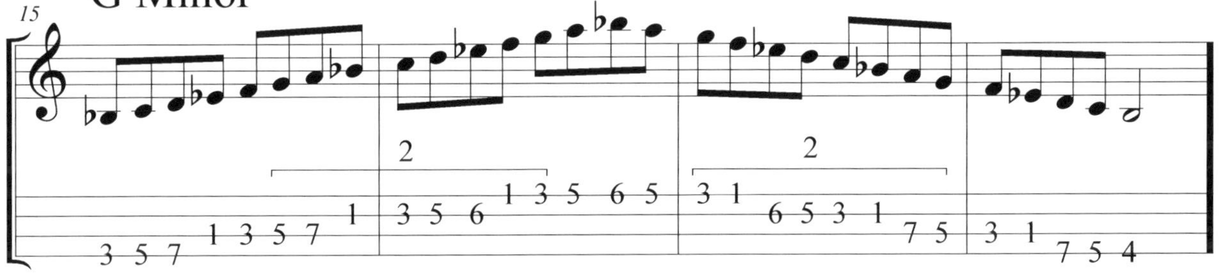

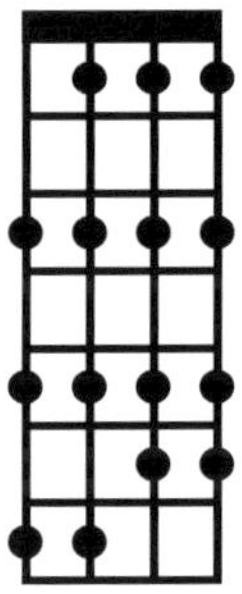

Practice Progression

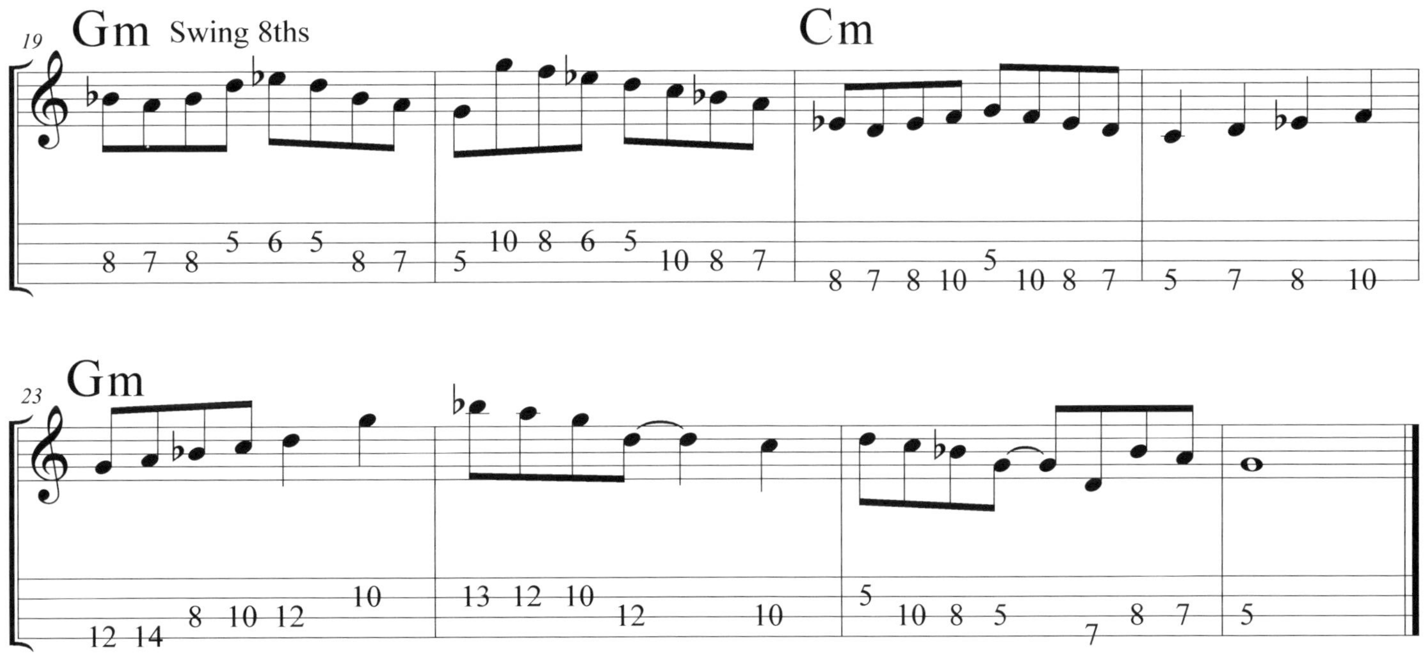

10. Mandolin Technique

Although this book is not meant to be a technique manual, let's look at some mandolin techniques and tricks that will help spice up your solos. Note: This chapter does not cover basic techniques such as slides, hammer-ons, pull-offs, and tremolo.

Drones

Drones on the mandolin can be defined as adding one or more continuous or recurring chord tones above or below the melody line to add thickness and resonance. They are often heard in fiddle tunes.

Drones sound best on open strings below the melody. You can figure out what drone to use by finding a chord tone outside the melody that matches the chord that is being played. Here is the A section of "Angeline the Baker" with simple drones added:

Double Stops

Double stops can be defined as playing two notes at once using any combination of chord tones across two adjacent strings. Whereas drones play a single note under multiple melody notes, double stops often change on every note along with the melody. If you look at your fretboard and visualize all of the chord tones, you can start to see where double stops are located. They are often played as long notes using tremolo, but can be used in many other ways. You can also create triple and quadruple stops, with 3 and 4 notes respectively. Here are some G-chord double stops:

G Double Stops

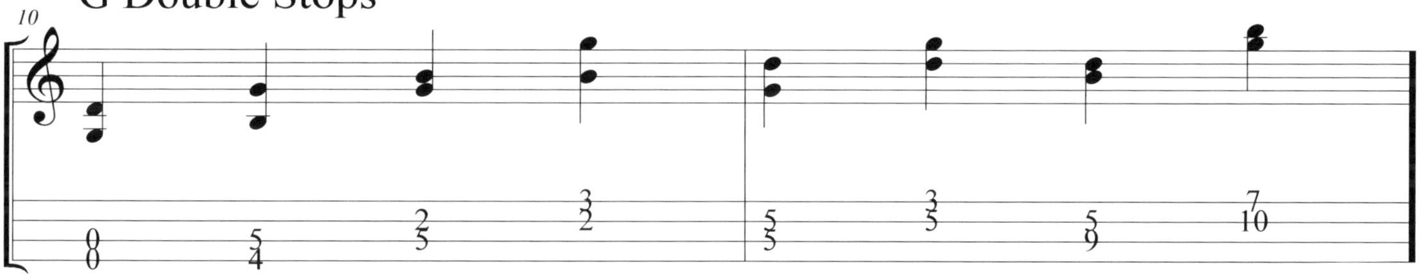

Double stops are often utilized to create a harmony line under the melody. Here is "Angeline the Baker" with a harmony line:

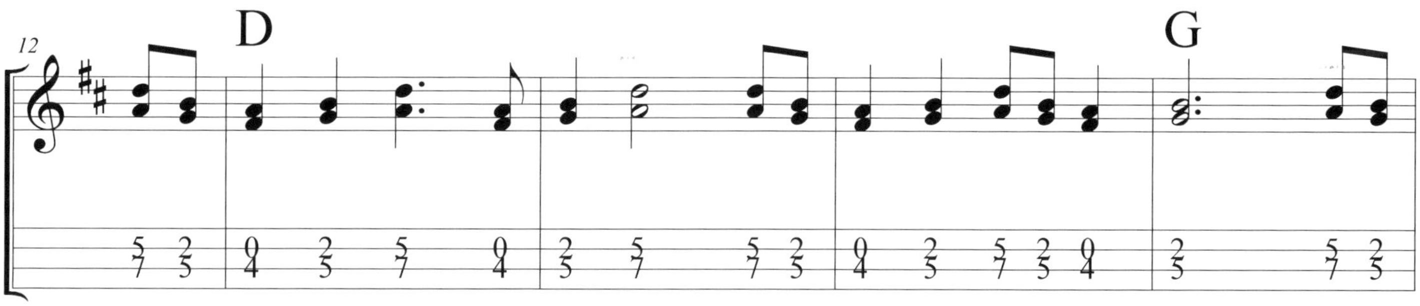

Rhythmic Picking and Cross Picking

Using chords, as well as double, triple and quadruple stops, you can play each note separately in different rhythmic patterns. Skipping a string in these patterns is known as **cross picking**. Using this technique in your solo can help make the mandolin sound "bigger" and is especially useful with minimal instrumentation and solo mandolin pieces. This technique also makes great practice material.

Here is an example:

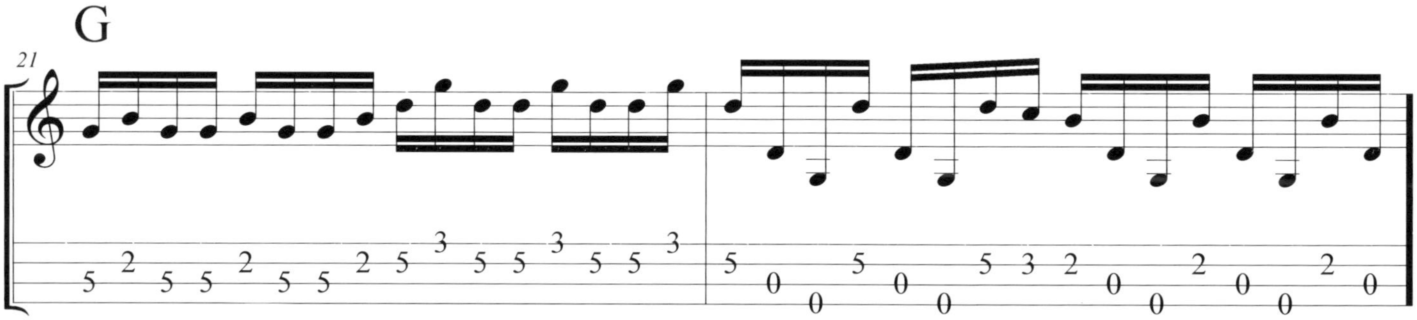

Here is a sample solo using all the techniques we have gone over in this chapter. Learn the solo and write your own. Be creative!

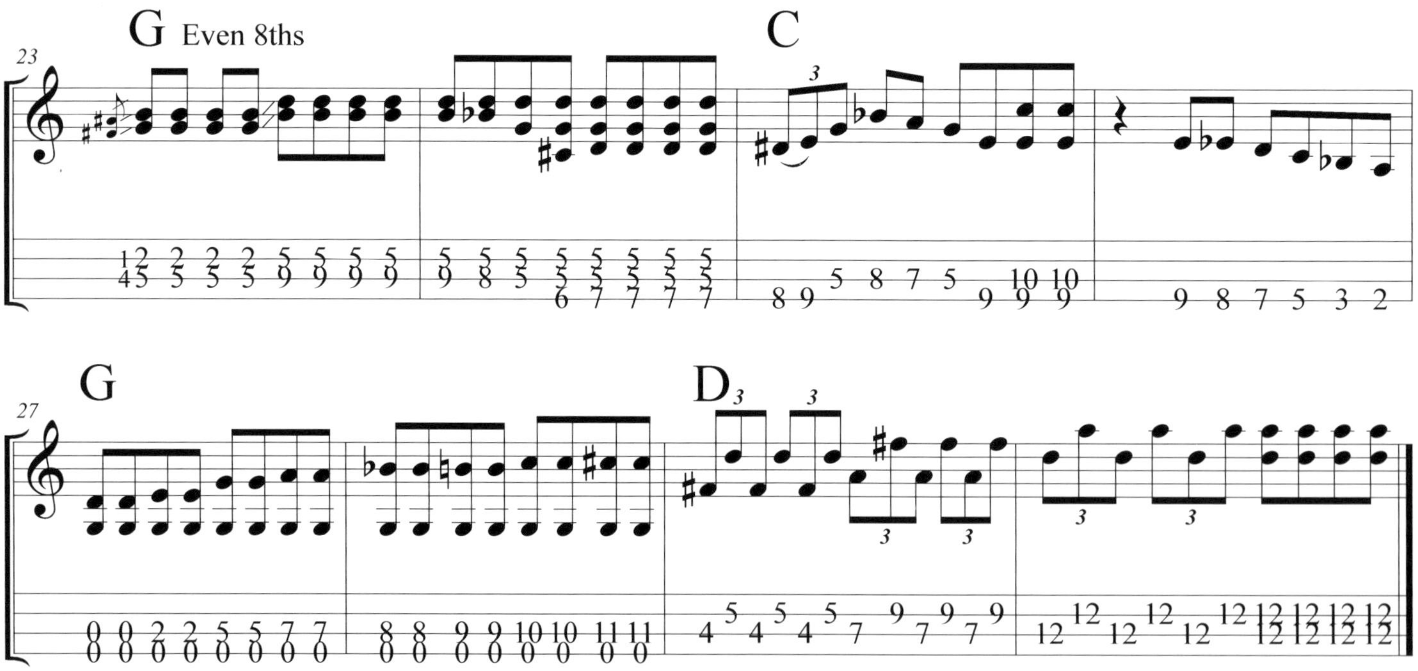

Appendix

Audio Practice Progressions-Keys and Track Numbers

Key Track

Practice Progression #1 - A - 26
Practice Progression #1 - B♭ - 27
Practice Progression #1 - B - 28
Practice Progression #1 - C - 29
Practice Progression #1 - D♭ - 30
Practice Progression #1 - D - 31
Practice Progression #1 - E♭ - 32
Practice Progression #1 - E - 33
Practice Progression #1 - F - 34
Practice Progression #1 - F♯ - 35
Practice Progression #1 - G - 36
Practice Progression #1 - A♭ - 37
Practice Progression #2 - A - 38
Practice Progression #2 - B♭ - 39
Practice Progression #2 - B - 40
Practice Progression #2 - C - 41
Practice Progression #2 - D♭ - 42
Practice Progression #2 - D - 43
Practice Progression #2 - E♭ - 44
Practice Progression #2 - E - 45
Practice Progression #2 - F - 46
Practice Progression #2 - F♯ - 47
Practice Progression #2 - G - 48
Practice Progression #2 - A♭ - 49
Practice Progression #3 - A - 50
Practice Progression #3 - B♭ - 51
Practice Progression #3 - B - 52
Practice Progression #3 - C - 53
Practice Progression #3 - D♭ - 54
Practice Progression #3 - D - 55

Key Track

Practice Progression #3 - E♭ - 56
Practice Progression #3 - E - 57
Practice Progression #3 - F - 58
Practice Progression #3 - F♯ - 59
Practice Progression #3 - G - 60
Practice Progression #3 - A♭ - 61
Practice Progression #4 - A - 62
Practice Progression #4 - B♭ - 63
Practice Progression #4 - B - 64
Practice Progression #4 - C - 65
Practice Progression #4 - D♭ - 66
Practice Progression #4 - D - 67
Practice Progression #4 - E♭ - 68
Practice Progression #4 - E - 69
Practice Progression #4 - F - 70
Practice Progression #4 - F♯ - 71
Practice Progression #4 - G - 72
Practice Progression #4 - A♭ - 73
Practice Progression #5 - Am - 74
Practice Progression #5 - B♭m - 75
Practice Progression #5 - Bm - 76
Practice Progression #5 - Cm - 77
Practice Progression #5 - D♭m - 78
Practice Progression #5 - Dm - 79
Practice Progression #5 - E♭m - 80
Practice Progression #5 - Em - 81
Practice Progression #5 - Fm - 82
Practice Progression #5 - F♯m - 83
Practice Progression #5 - Gm - 84
Practice Progression #5 - A♭m - 85

Major Keys

Triads in C Major and Sharp-Bearing Keys

Major Keys

Triads in C Major and Flat-Bearing Keys

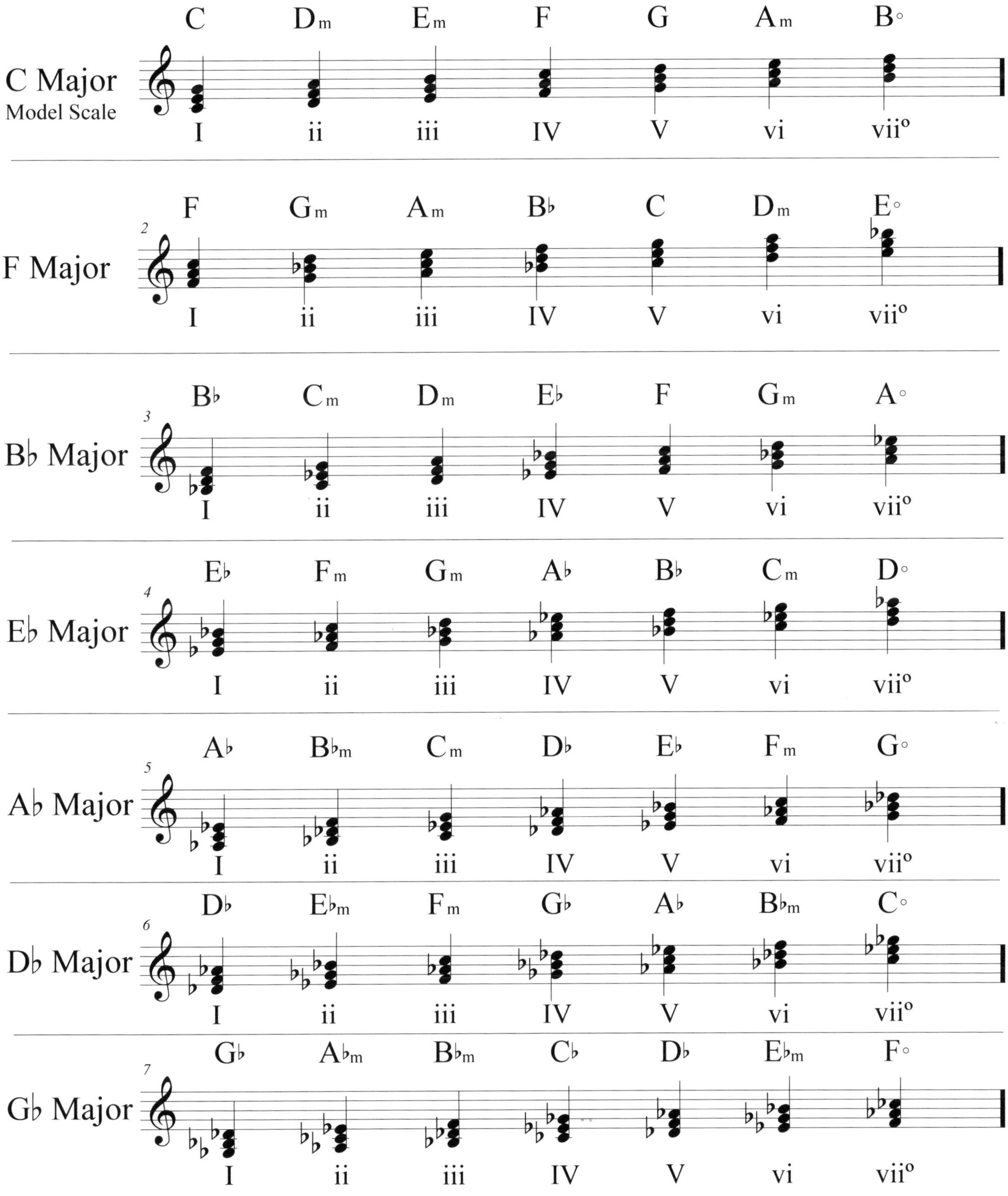

Major Scale and Pentatonic Relationship

If you take the IV and V Chords of a key and play their respective major scales, they will conflict with the overall key. Below, you can see the conflicting notes (marked with a X) in the key of C that appear in the G and F major scales.

C Major Scale (I)

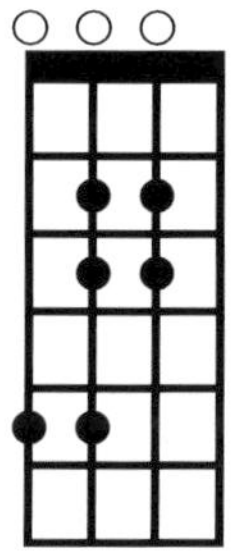

F Major Scale (IV) G Major Scale (V)

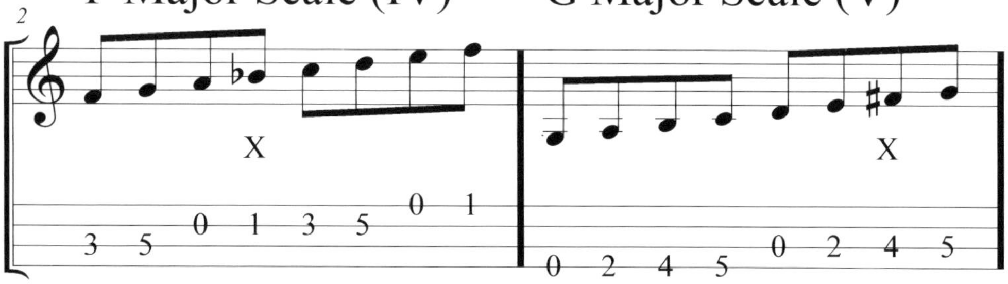

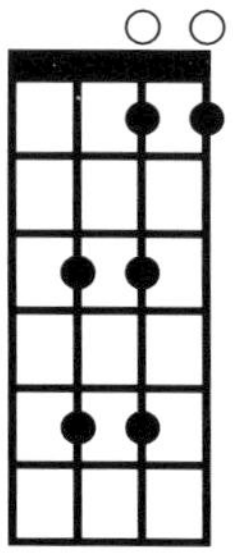

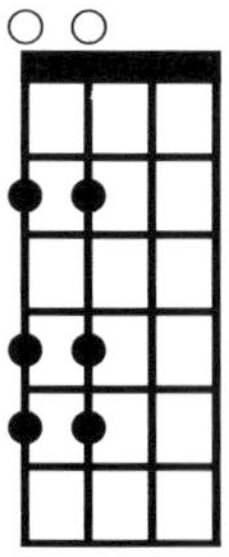

When you play pentatonic scales instead, each conflicting note is omitted and each scale fits into the overall key of C. This way you can change pentatonic scales with each chord change and still play within the key.

C Pentatonic Scale (I)

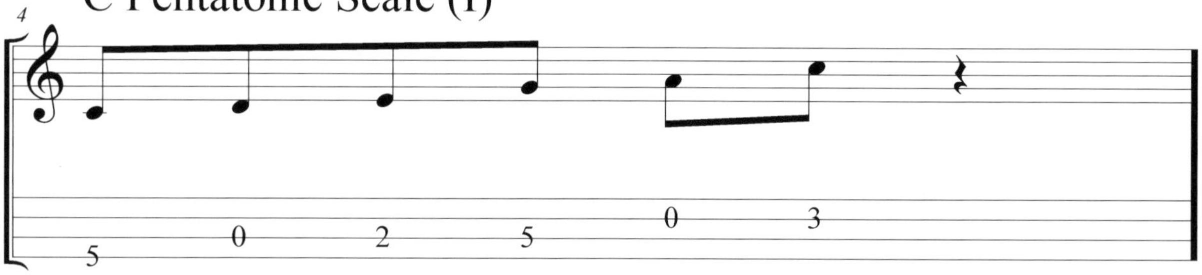

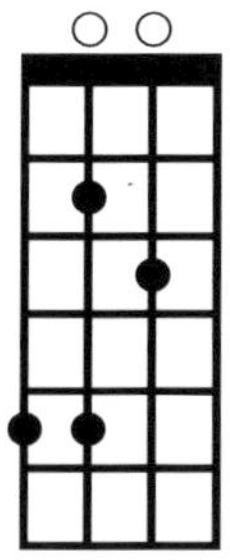

F Pentatonic Scale (IV) G Pentatonic Scale (V)

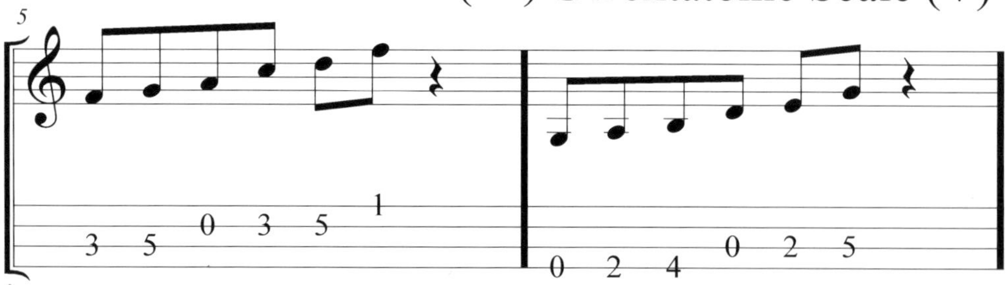

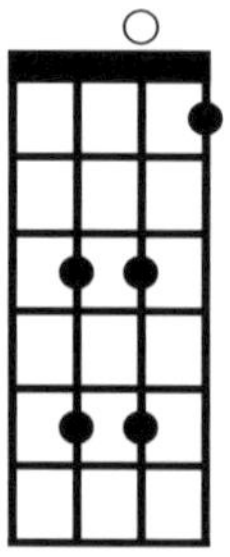

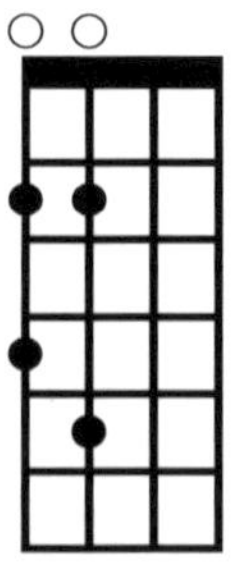

Open-Position Chord Tones

Major Triads

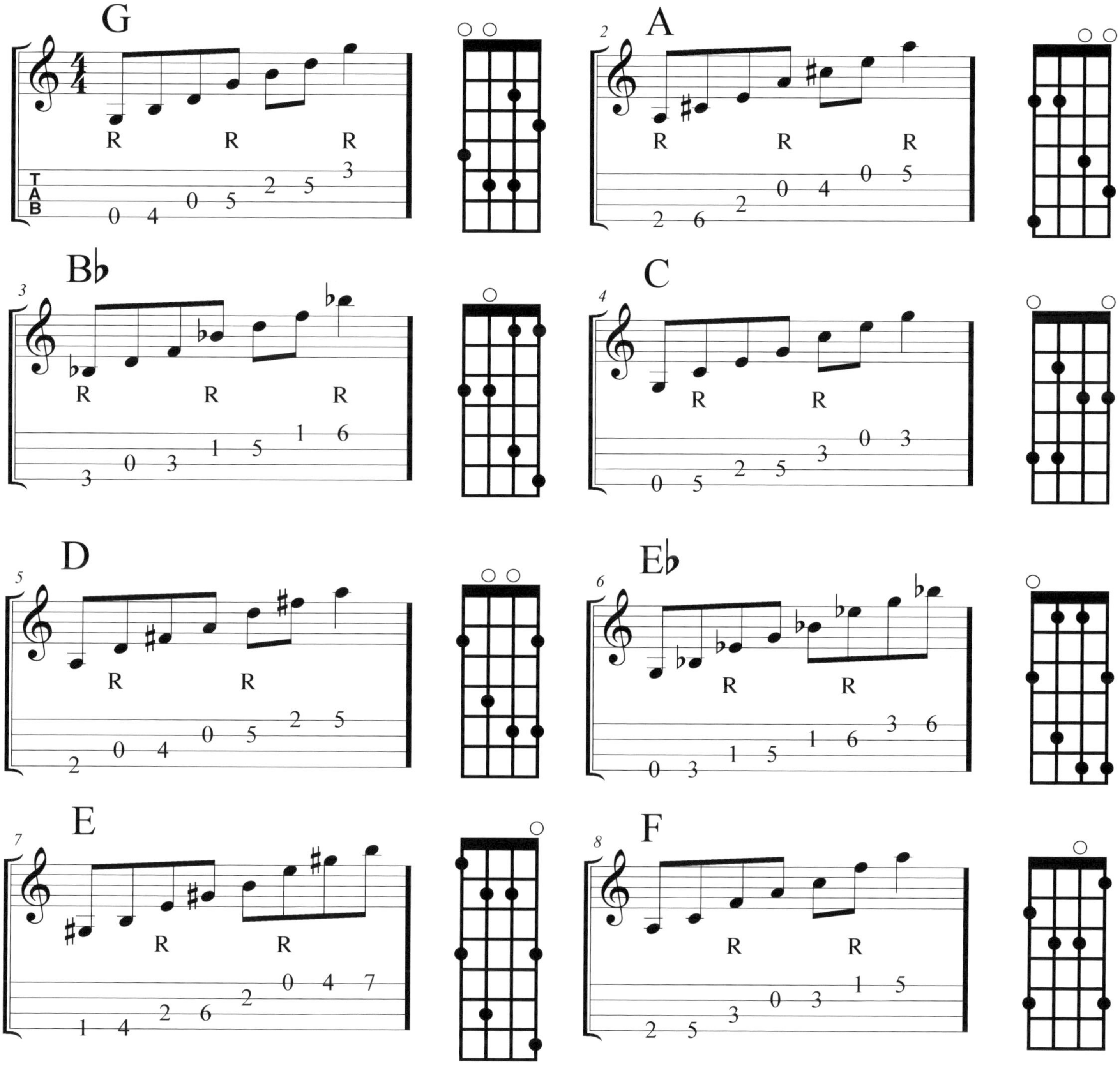

Minor Triads

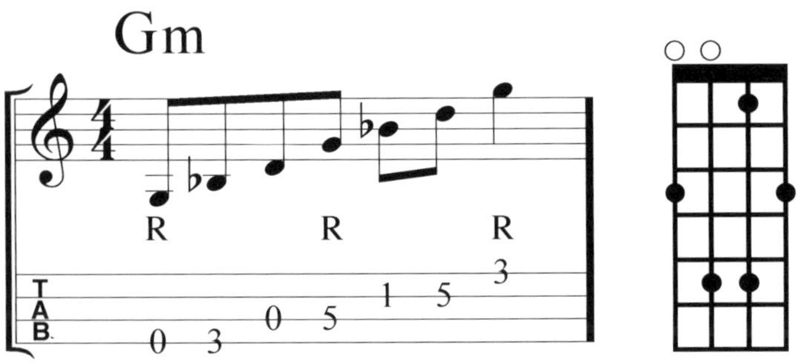

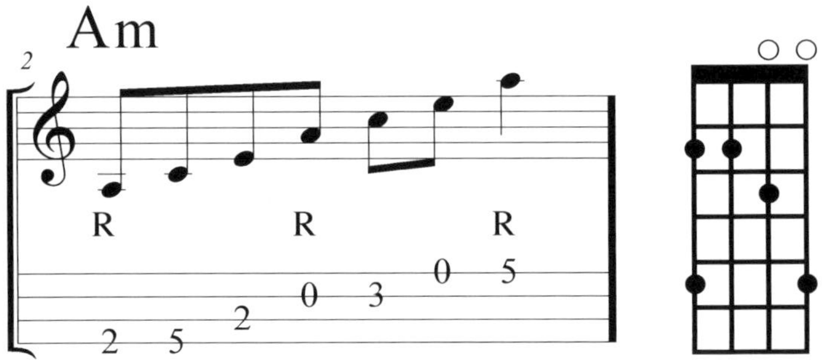

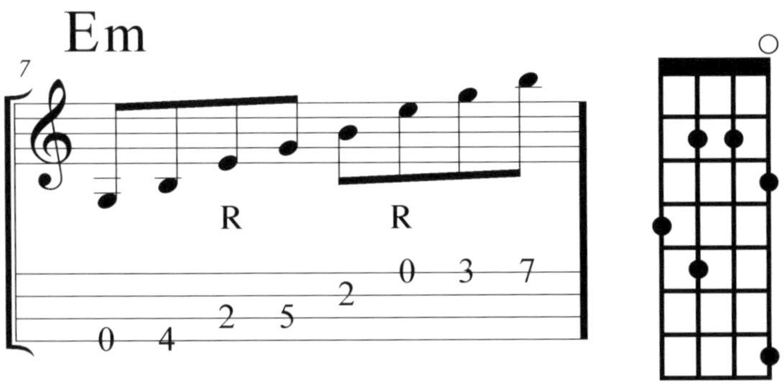

Dominant 7ths

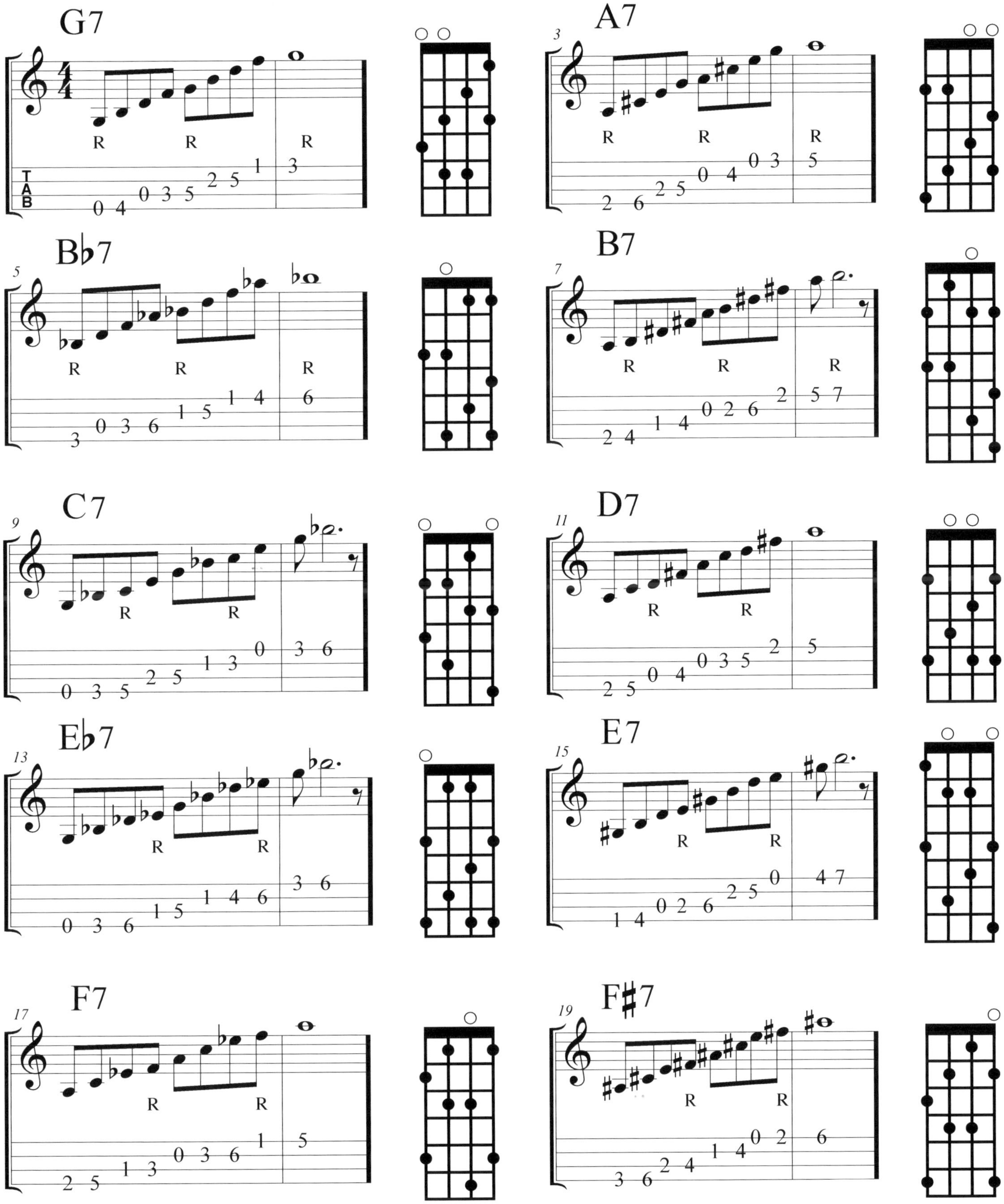

Arpeggio Boxes

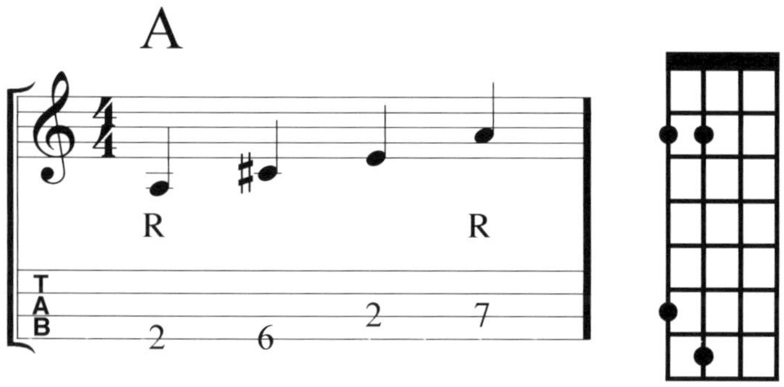

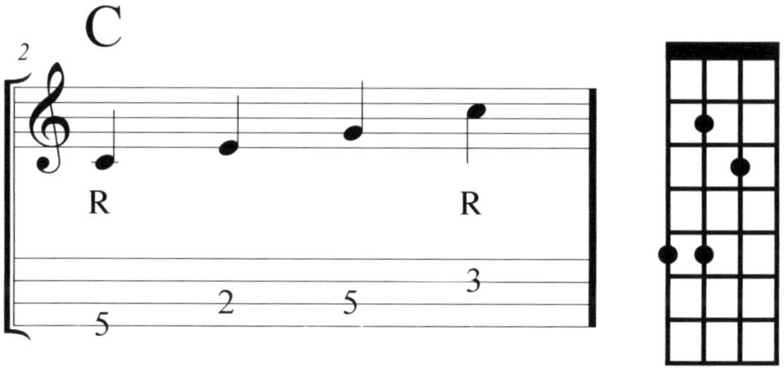

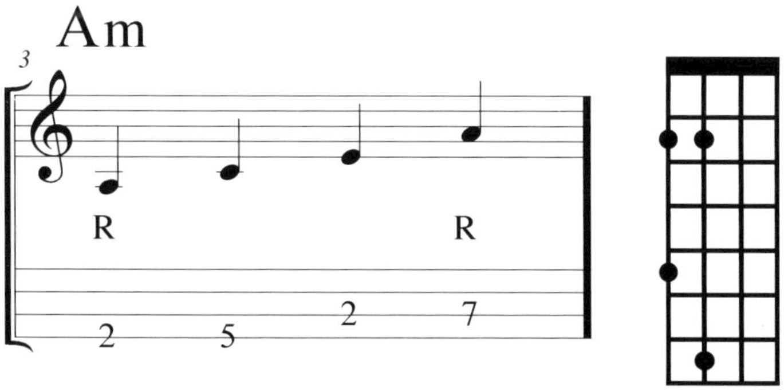

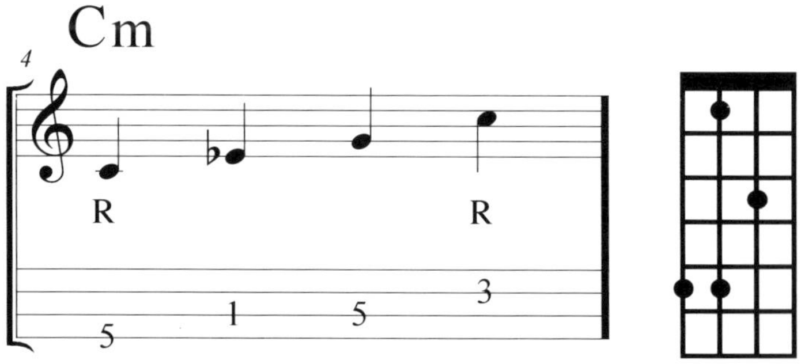

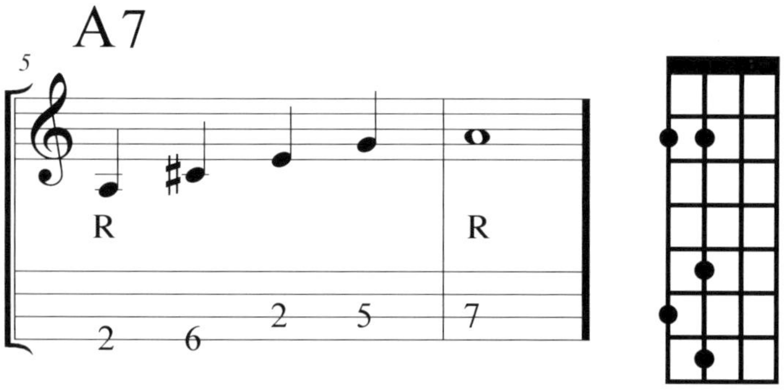

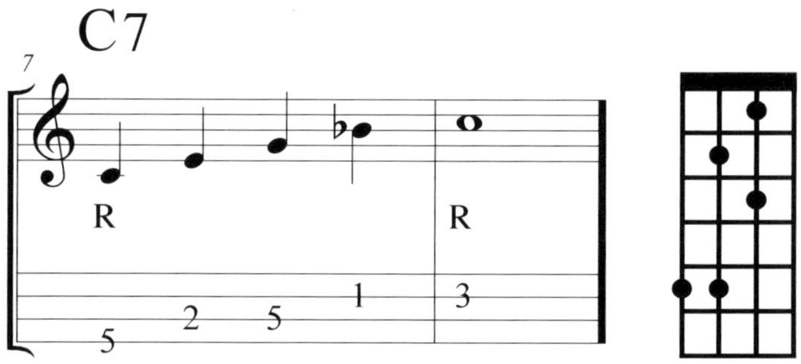

Open-Position Scales

Major Pentatonic Scales

G

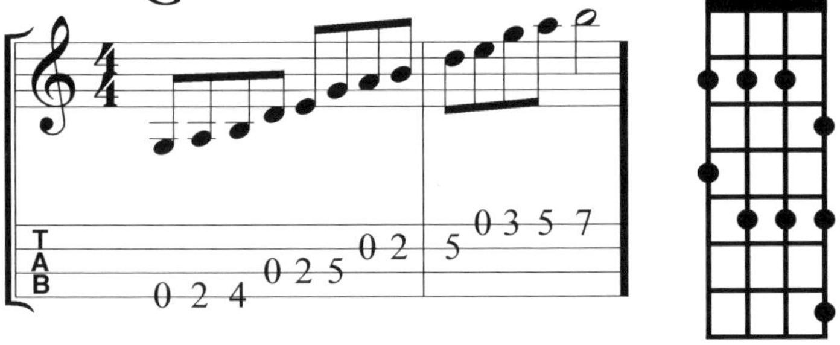

A

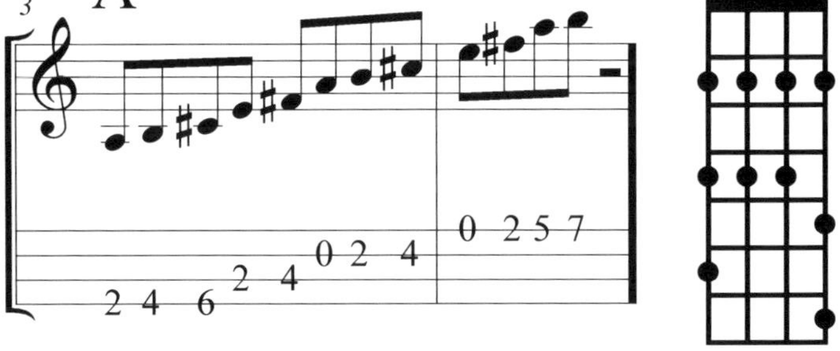

B♭ (A♯)

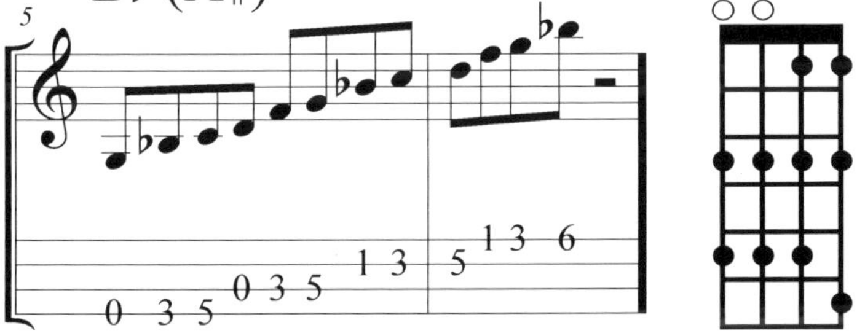

C

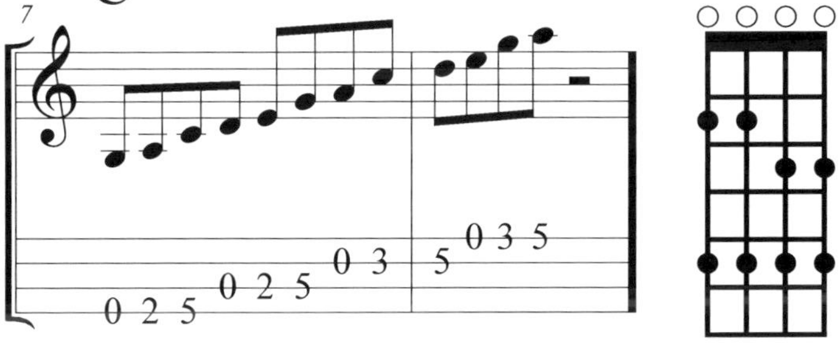

D

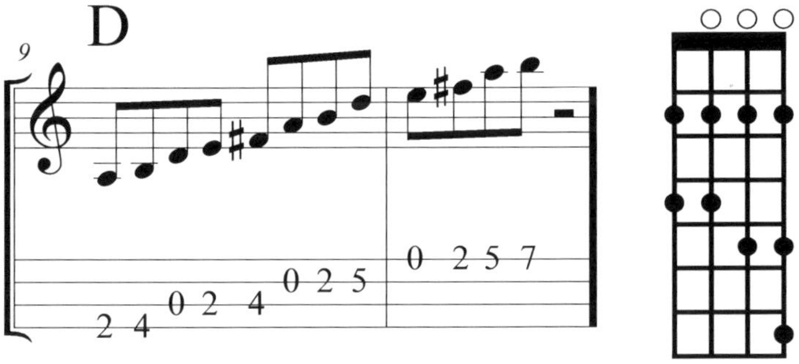

E♭ (D♯)

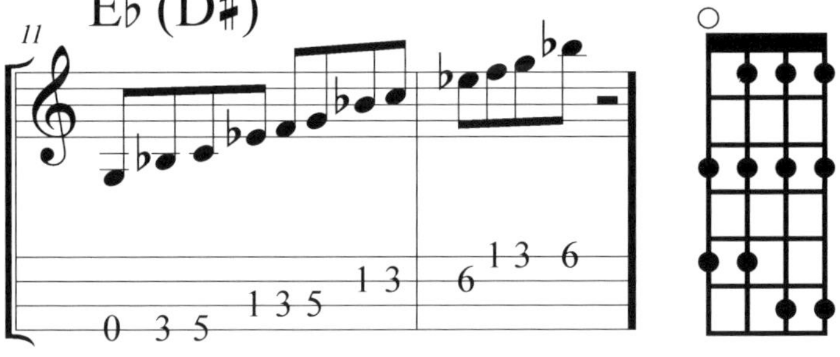

E

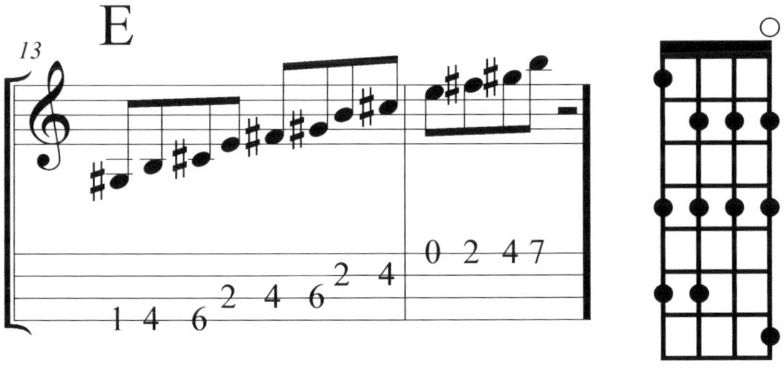

F

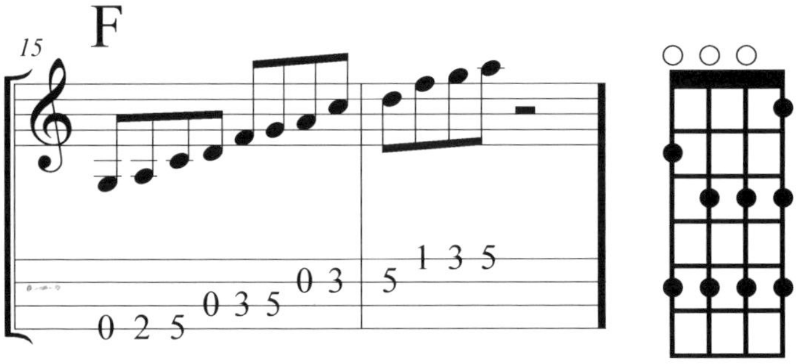

Minor Pentatonic Scales

G

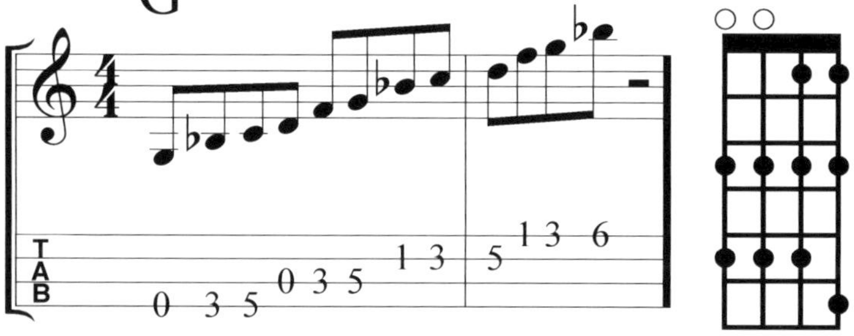

A

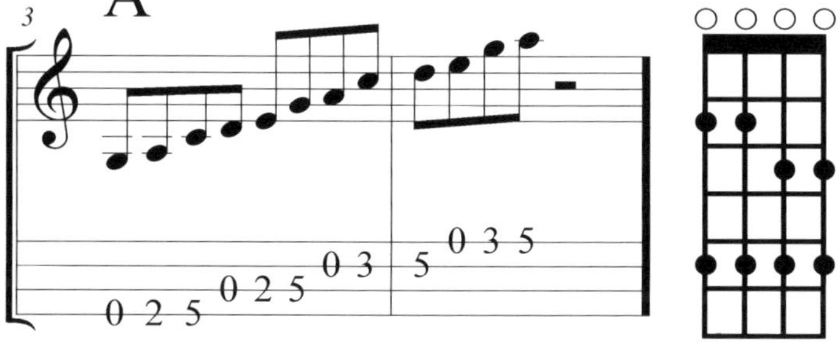

B

C

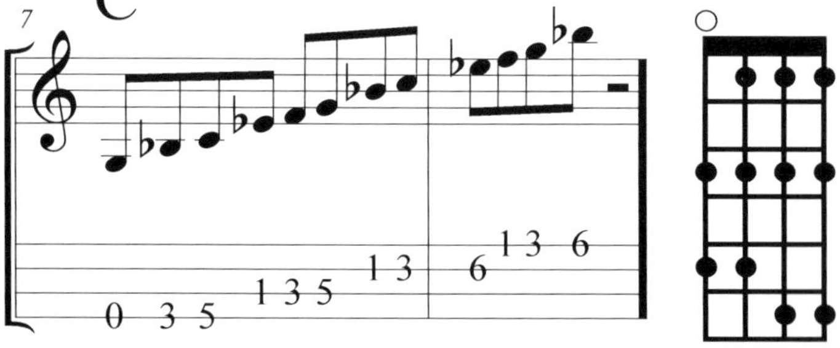

C♯ (D♭)

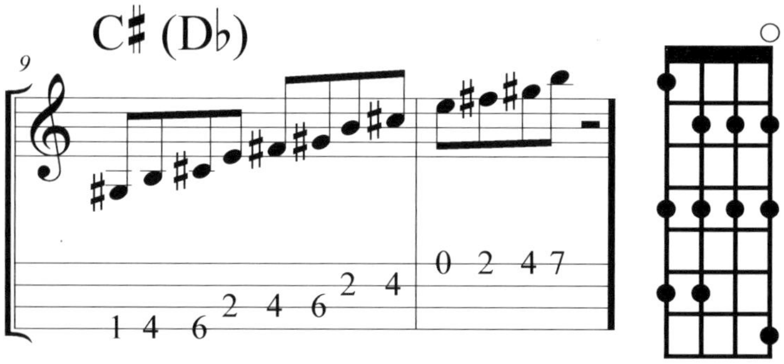

D

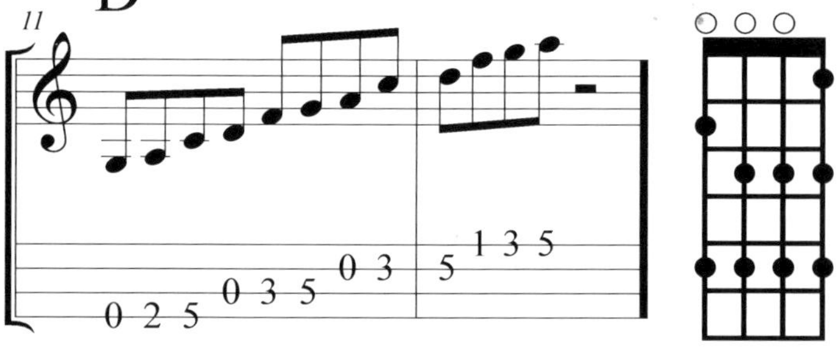

E

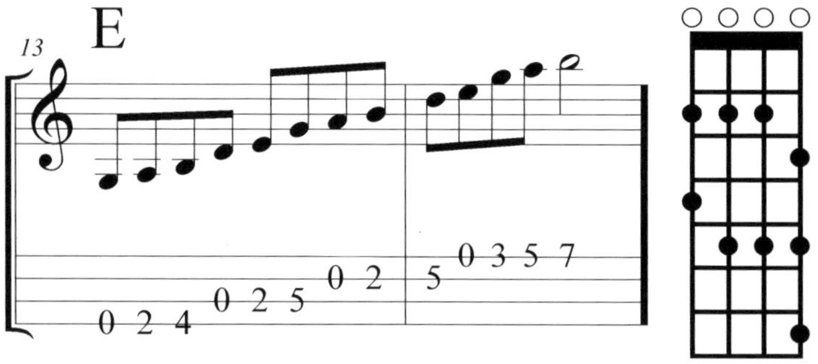

F♯ (G♭)

Major Scales

G

A♭ (G♯)

A

B♭ (A♯)

B

Major Scales Continued

C

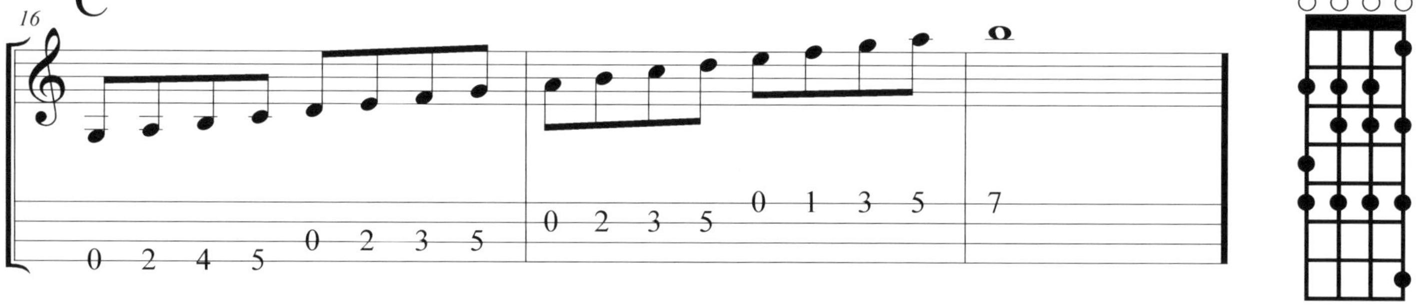

D

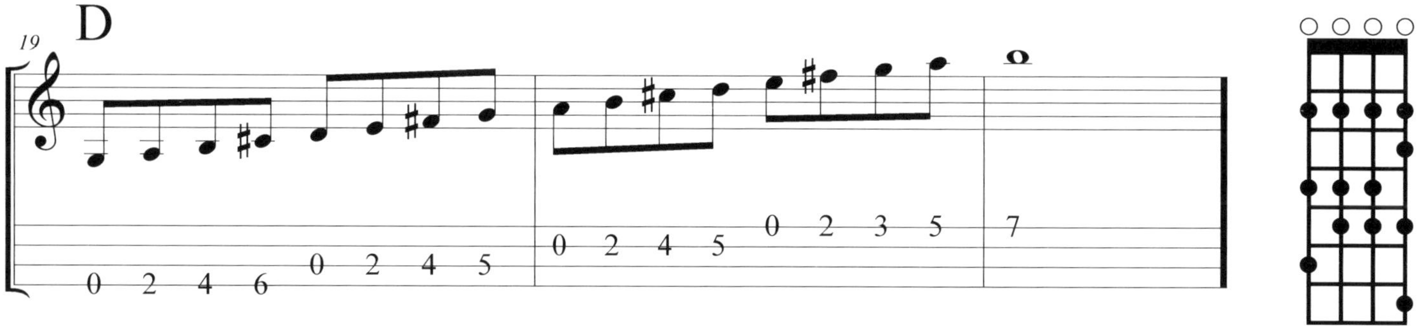

E♭ (D♯)

E

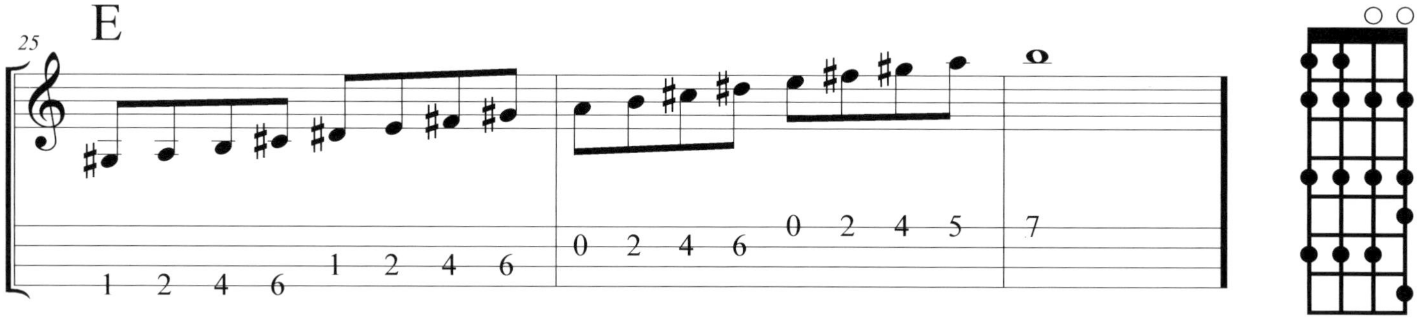

F

Natural Minor Scales

G

G♯ (A♭)

A

B

C

Natural Minor Scales Continued

C♯ (D♭)

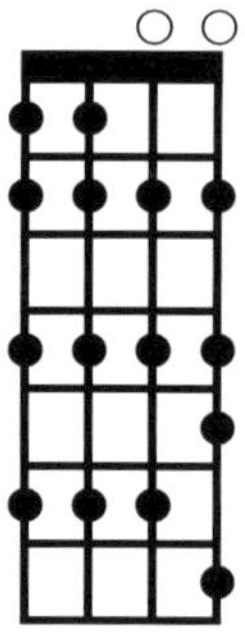

D

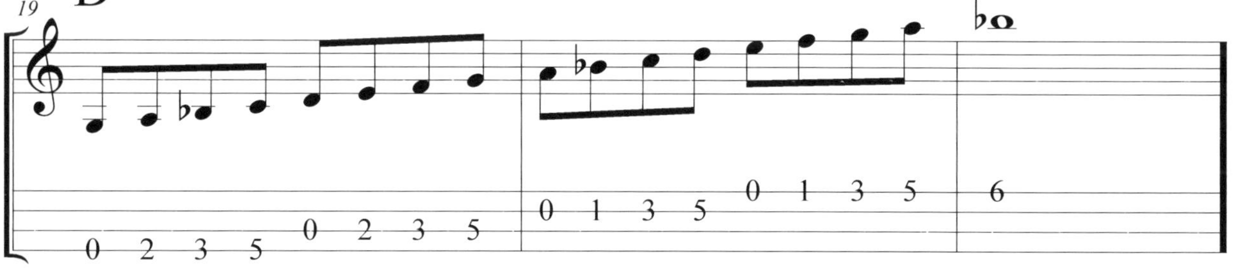

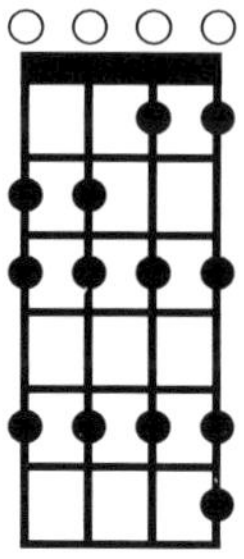

E

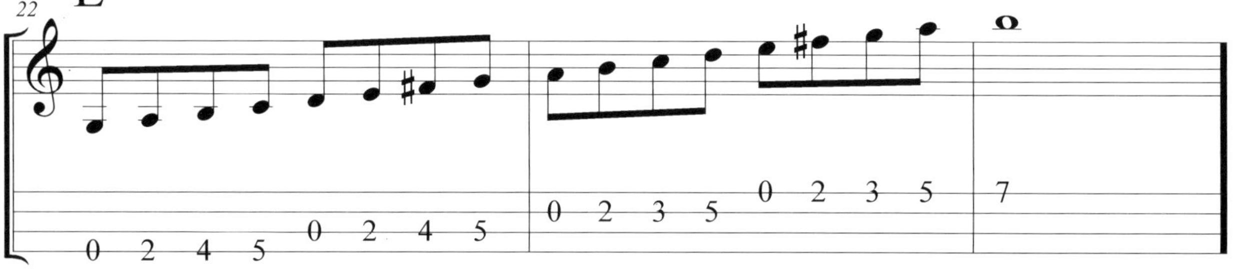

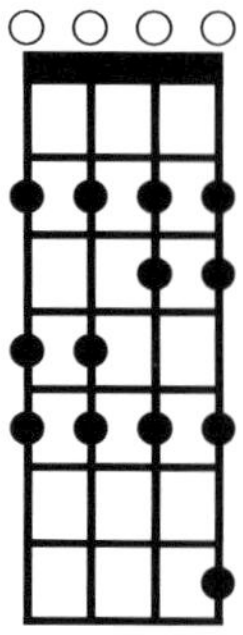

F

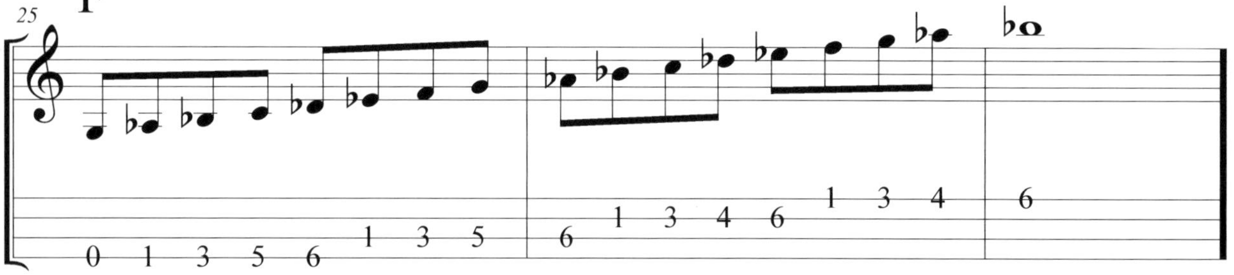

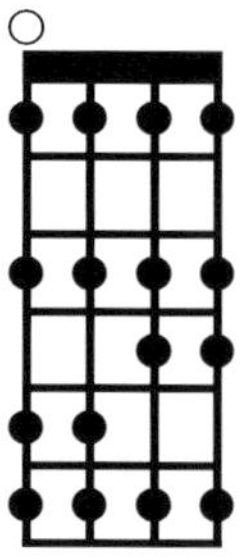

F♯ (G♭)

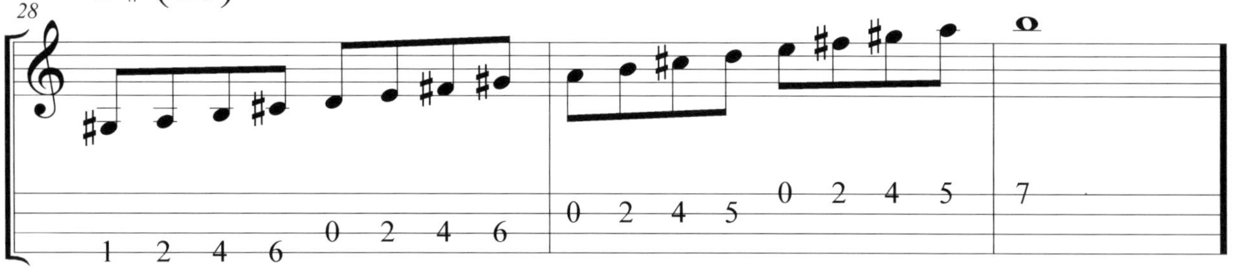

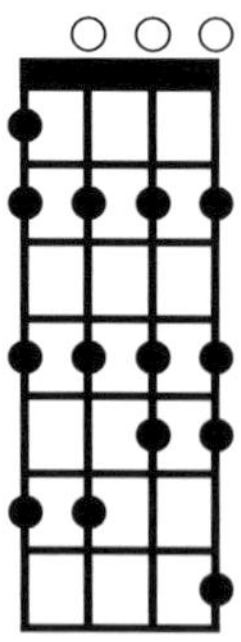

Basic Scales: Scale Boxes

A Major Pentatonic Scale Box 1

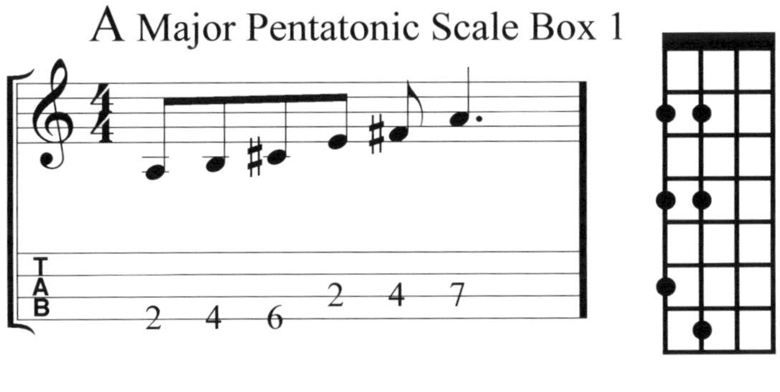

C Major Pentatonic Scale Box 2

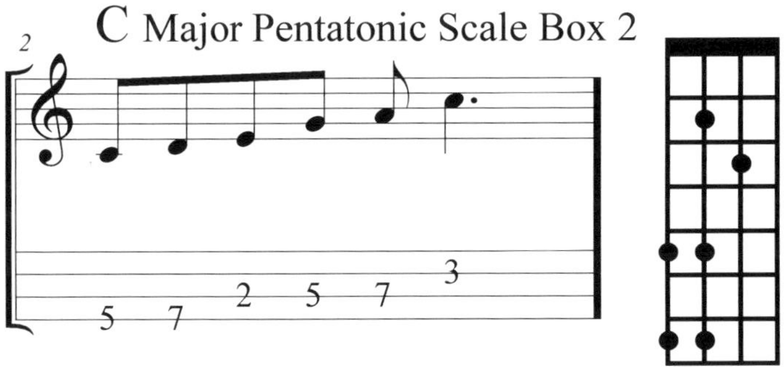

A Minor Pentatonic Scale Box 1

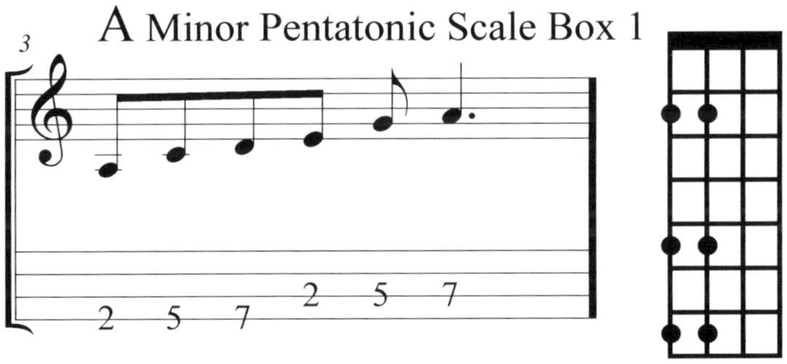

C Minor Pentatonic Scale Box 2

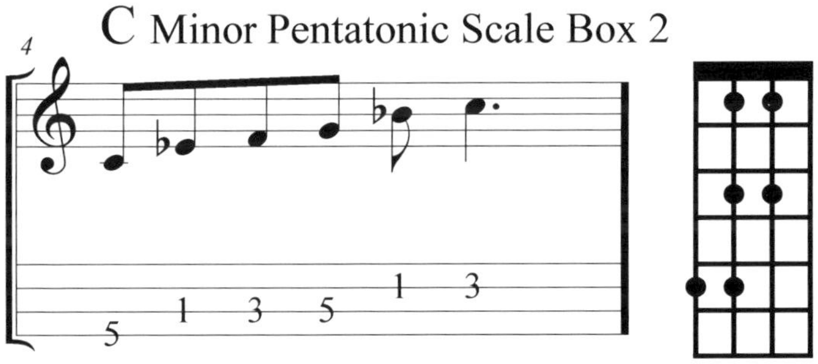

A Major Scale Box 1

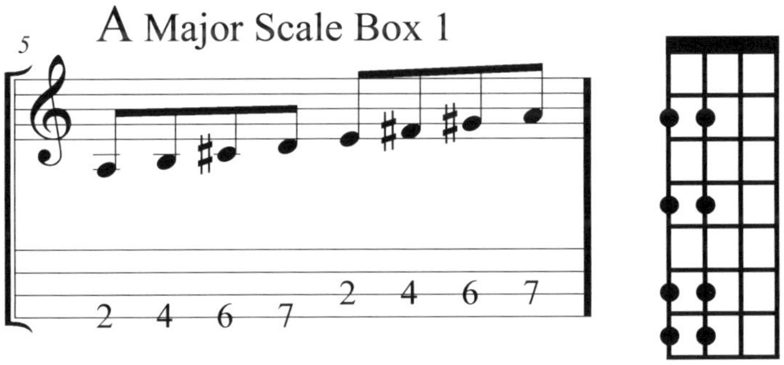

C Major Scale Box 2

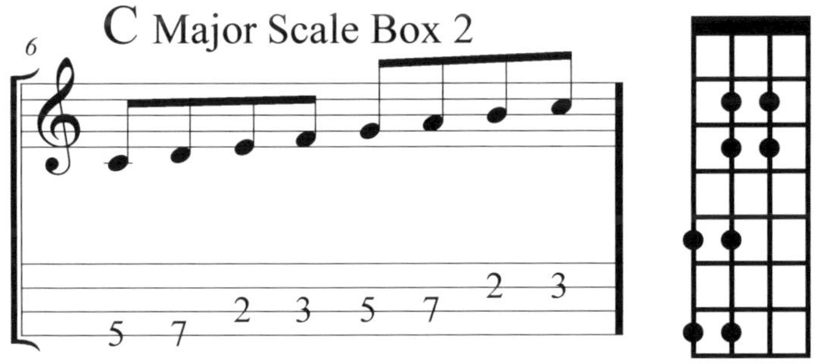

A Natural Minor Scale Box 1

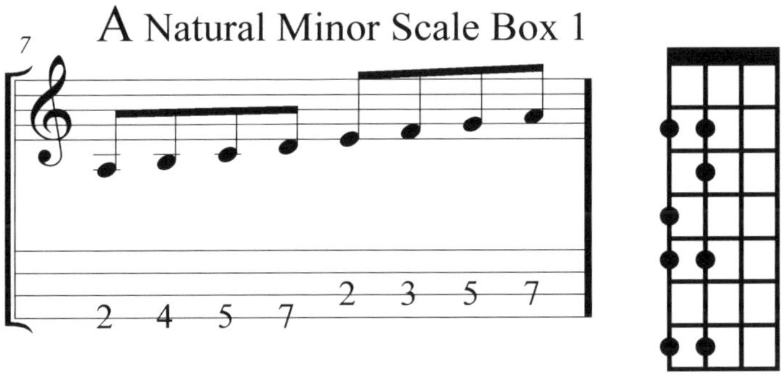

C Natural Minor Scale Box 2

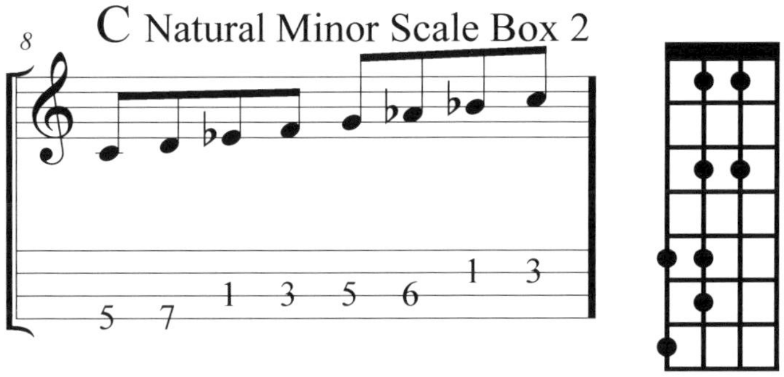

Practice Progressions

The next few pages feature 5 different progressions for you to practice improvising. Each progression is written in Roman numerals, and has a corresponding recorded track in every key. These progressions are very common in all styles of music, and are a great way to not only practice improvisation, but to also learn the chords represented by Roman numerals in each key.

1.

26-37

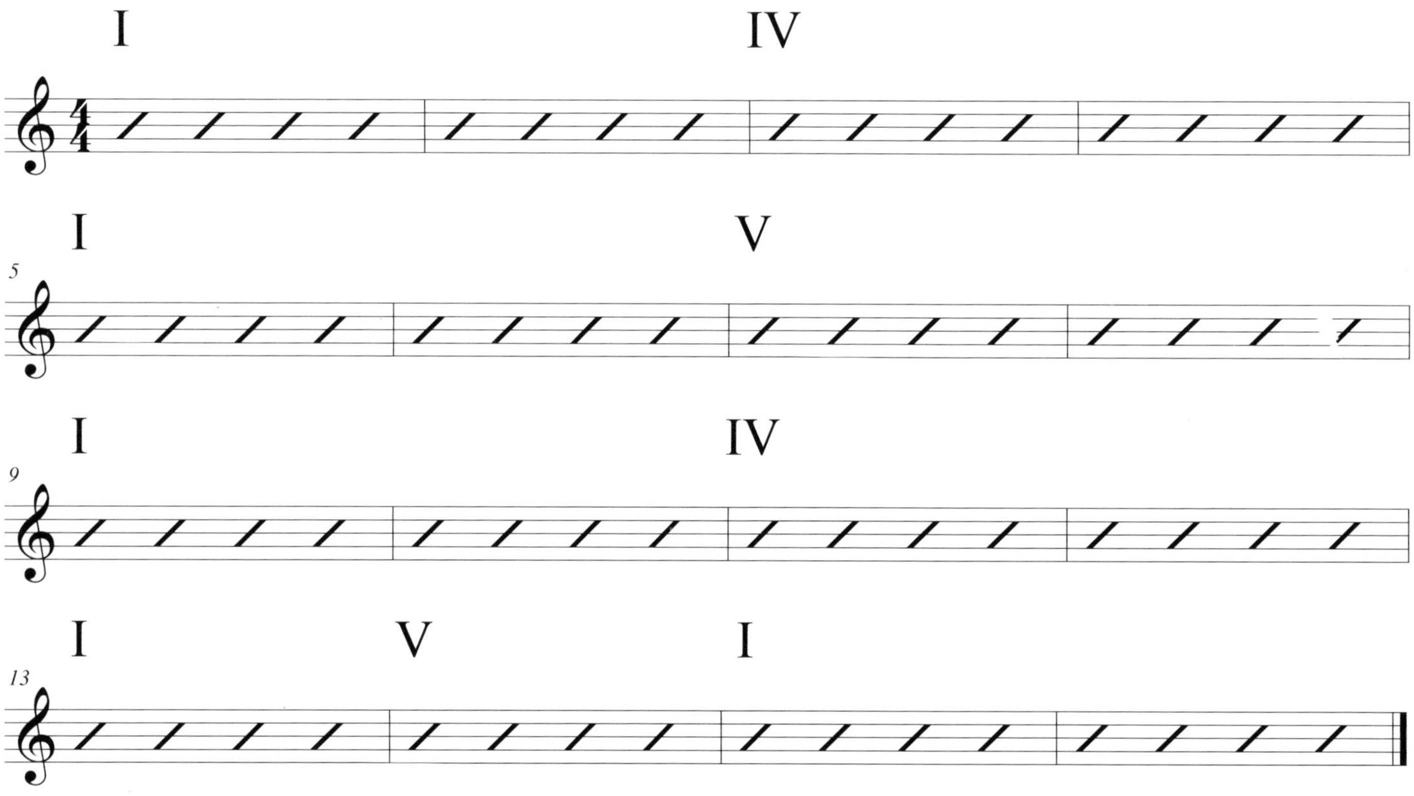

Practice Progressions Continued

2.

38-49

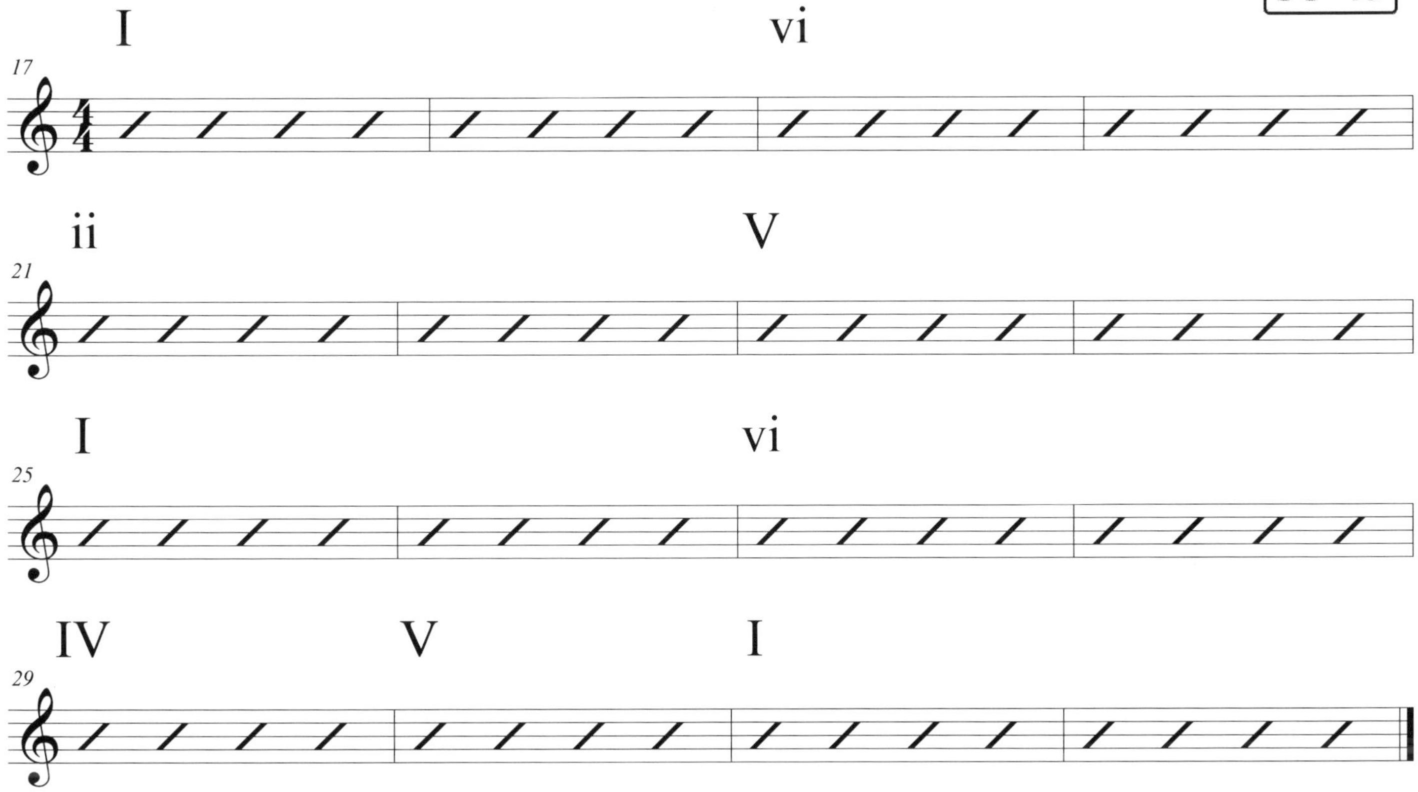

3.

50-61

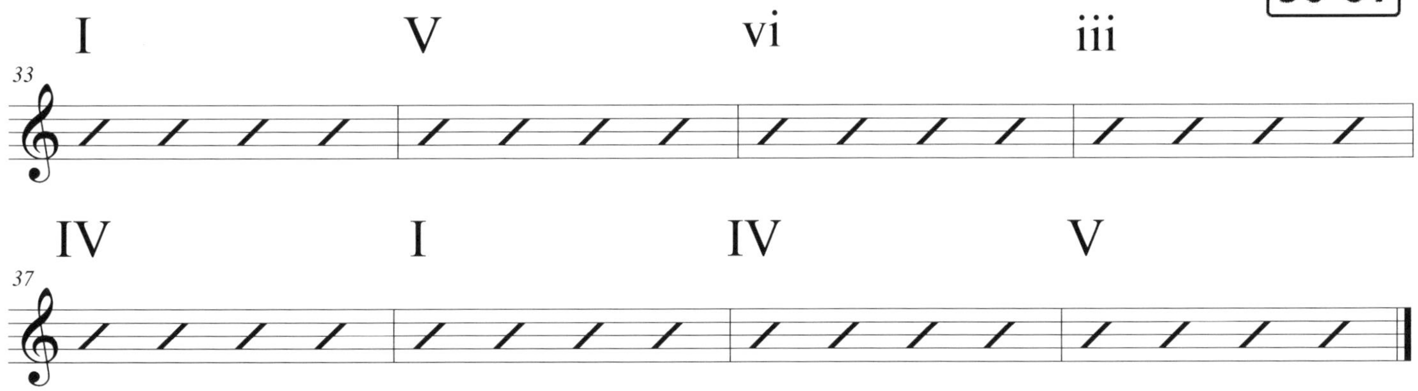

Practice Progressions Continued

4.

62-73

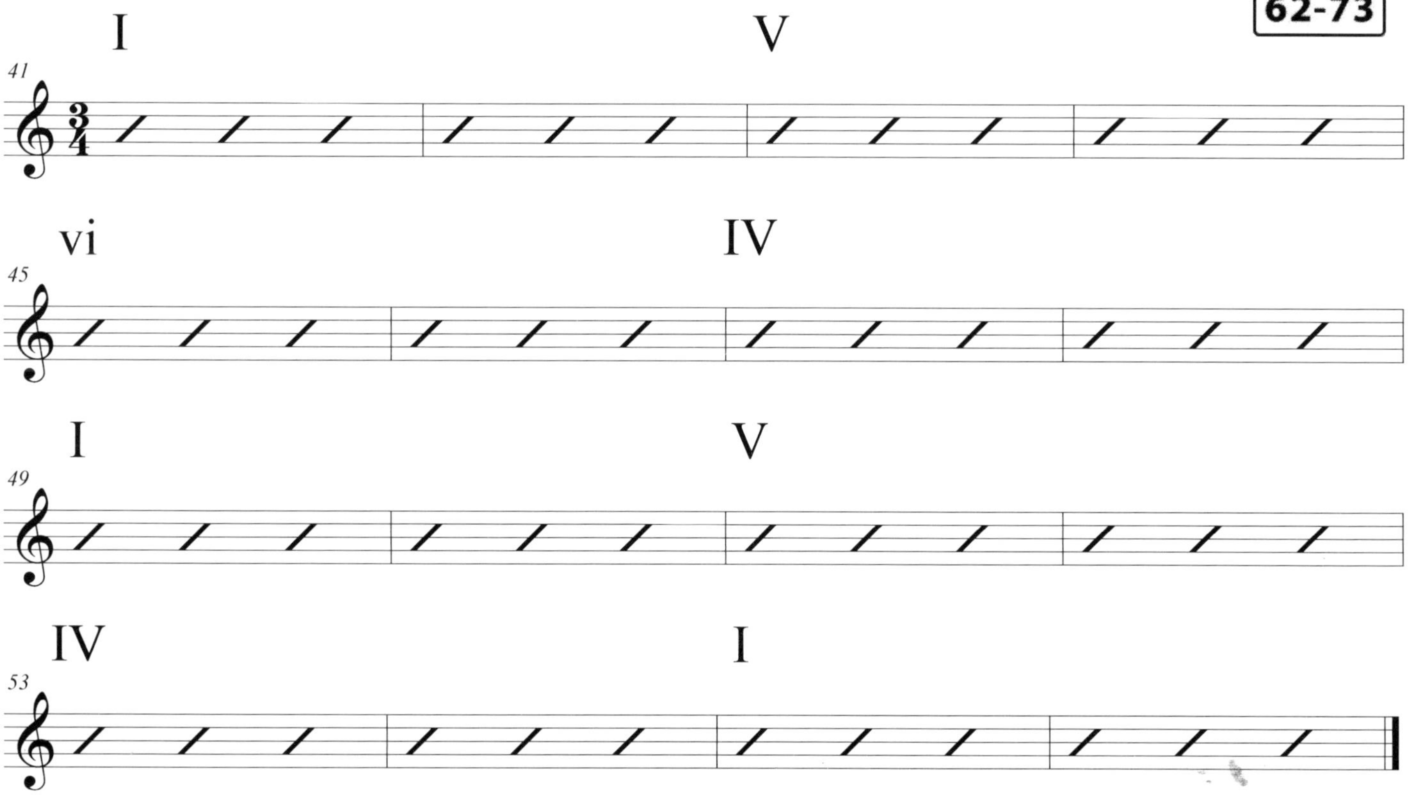

5.

74-85

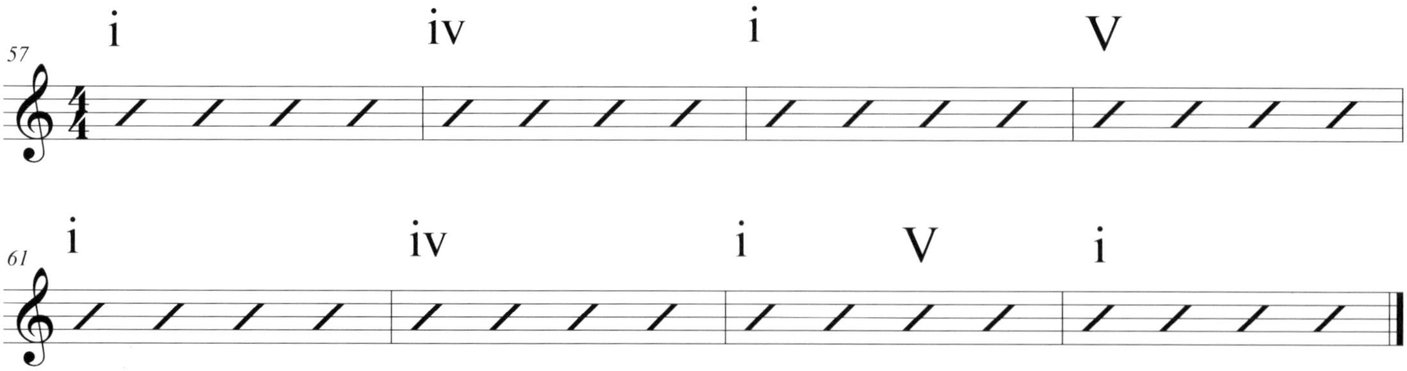